checked Nov-11

い卩

# Bull Terriers

*Ch. Arguside Yuletide Ghoste on Curraneye.*

# BULL TERRIERS

## AN OWNER'S COMPANION

## Robin Salyn

The Crowood Press

First published in 1989 by
The Crowood Press
Ramsbury, Marlborough,
Wiltshire SN8 2HE

British Library Cataloguing in Publication Data

Robin Salyn
  Bull terriers: an owner's companion
  I. Title
  636.7'55

  ISBN 1–85223–142–4

**Acknowledgements**
Photographs on pages 8, 14, 26, 102, 158, 166, 175 and 176 by
Robin Salyn; pages 17, 18, 31, 129, 139 and 167 by Derrik James;
pages 52, 94, 95 and 107 by Legend Financial Communications;
page 55 by M. Cox; pages 98, 101, 104, 106 and 110 by G. Jackson;
page 109 by J. Mildenhall; pages 111, 119 and 120 by R. and A.
Edmonds; page 121 by Mrs R. Seddon; pages 144, 146 and 147 by
Peter John. Frontispiece by Dave Freeman.
Line-drawings by Aileen Hanson
Breed standards reproduced by kind permission of the Kennel
Club of Great Britain and The American Kennel Club

Typeset by Acorn Bookwork, Salisbury, Wiltshire
Printed in Great Britain at The Bath Press

# Contents

|   | Introduction | 7 |
| 1 | Conformation and Characteristics | 11 |
| 2 | The Bull Terrier Puppy | 28 |
| 3 | Socialisation | 40 |
| 4 | Training an Adolescent Dog | 50 |
| 5 | Mature Bull Terriers | 60 |
| 6 | Showing | 72 |
| 7 | Entering a Show – The Preliminaries | 82 |
| 8 | At the Show | 97 |
| 9 | Breeding and Mating | 117 |
| 10 | Care of the Pregnant Bitch | 138 |
| 11 | Whelping | 153 |
| 12 | Rearing | 164 |
|   | Appendix 1 | 178 |
|   | Appendix 2 | 179 |
|   | Appendix 3 | 181 |
|   | Appendix 4 | 183 |
|   | Bibliography | 188 |
|   | Index | 189 |

# Introduction

To be as one with your Bull Terrier it helps to be able to understand the reasons for his actions – not only his general canine instincts, but the more individual characteristics of the Bull Terrier inherited from the various breeds that have gone into his making. Bull Terriers are the result of cross-breeding between bulldogs and terriers, and were initially known as 'Bull-and-Terriers' or 'Bulldog Terriers'. They were the realisation of attempts by early bull- and bear-baiting enthusiasts to improve the tenacity and speed of their dogs. Similar cross-breeding exercises are taking place today, in America, in an effort to develop a strain of American Pit Bull Terriers.

The original bulldog was renowned for his courage and had been used in bear- and bull-baiting. The English Terrier, either black and tan, or white (now extinct), was at once a house companion and vermin hunter, and was going out of fashion by the mid-nineteenth century, being of rather uncertain temperament and very free with his teeth! Early illustrations show the results of their cross-breeding looking more like bulldogs than terriers. They appear to have come in all the colours found in Bull Terriers today. It was soon discovered by breeders that the cross between them should only be a quarter or at most half, bulldog, as if there was more than half, the resulting progeny tended to be heavy and slow, too undershot to be able to keep a firm grip with his teeth and too wilful to obey his trainer.

Judging by early illustrations and accounts from the period, early attempts at cross-breeding produced unbalanced animals with short thick heads, blunt muzzles, loose lips, thick-set muscles and bow legs. It was with the gamest of these that James Hinks experimented until he had bred longer-necked, alert, plucky gentlemen – a strain he called the 'Bull Terrier'. One of the best balanced was Ch. Marquis weighing fifty pounds (twenty-five kilograms). Gradually, there developed a dog with the longer stronger head, courage and

The Bull Terrier.

single-mindedness of the bulldog, but the agility of the terrier. They had the speed and tenacity to fight larger vermin such as the badger and fox or other fighting dogs, and yet were known to be excellently tempered companions. There is some controversy as to whether the Dalmation was used in developing the breed, but this cannot be so given their characteristics and colouring.

For many years, white was the preferred colour for Bull Terriers, but the coloured dog did survive in the Staffordshire area and finally received Kennel Club recognition in 1933. However, their introduction was not without problem, as they seemed to possess more of the less desirable bull characteristics. Even colour-bred whites (white puppies in a litter from coloured parents), were frowned upon by the pure-bred white fraternity – the Bull Terrier Club opened a stud book register for pure-bred whites. However, all whites have been considered equal since 1950.

The painful and futile practice of ear-cropping for bull terriers continued in Britain until 1895 (1956 in America). It was thought that it would be more difficult for the dog's adversary to gain a hold of, or tear the ear, making it bleed profusely, if it was cropped to a fine up-standing point; but if they were cropped incorrectly, or if the ears were not tended during the healing process, they became an ugly disfigurement and the scabs caused puckering. Nevertheless, any ears left uncropped were considered ugly, and after the Kennel Club banned the practice, efforts were made to breed animals with neat upright ears. The first of these – the 'Bloomsbury Charlewood' – was produced by Mr H.E. Monk.

Men apparently dominated the early stages of the Bull Terrier's development, and it was not until the era of the Canine Show that the ladies came to the fore. At the turn of the twentieth century, Mrs Olive Millner was both exhibiting and judging the breed, and Mrs Monk, wife of H.E. Monk of Bloomsbury fame, did much for the breed in America. Later came such renowned names as Granny Adlam, Miss Montague Johnson (Romany), Miss Joan Previtt (Kowhai) and Miss Eva Weatherill of Souperlative fame, to mention only a small proportion of those dedicated to the continued improvement of the breed. Miss Violet Drummond Dick bred the latest Bull Terrier to become Supreme Champion at Cruft's – Abraxas Audacity, 1972.

Nowadays, we have to thank Mr R.H. Oppenheimer C.B.E. and Miss Eva Weatherill for their foresight and determination in furthering the breed without detriment to the original character and temperament, make or shape, of the vision held by the earlier doyens of the Bull Terrier breed. In 1987, the Kennel Club made it possible for Breed Clubs to safeguard 'Historically Significant Affixes in their Breed'. The Bull Terrier Club took advantage of this to ensure that the following remained the sole property of the breed:

**Brendon** (Mrs Gladys M. Adlam)
**Contango** (Mrs Joy Schuster)
**Gardenia** (Mr and Mrs H.W. Potter)
**Kowhai** (Mrs Joan Previtt)
**Ormandy** (R.H. Oppenheiner C.B.E.)
**Regent** (Dr Geoffrey M. Vevers)
**Velhurst** (Mrs S. Philips)

It is clear that the Bull Terrier is a man-made breed, and it is up to the breeders of the future to carry on the excellent work. They must build on the work of their forebears to further improve this courageous, gallant, fun-loving gladiator of the canine race.

# 1

# Conformation and Characteristics

'Breeders had begun to breed more intelligently. In the 1920s Bull Terriers were really total cripples! Good movement came in during Champion Ormandy's McGuffin and Champion Velhurst Vindicator's time. Much of this was the result of Dr Vever's (Regent) influence. His dogs could move! People began to go to the dog that suited their bitch rather than to the latest Champion.

The qualities nowadays? The Bull Terriers have all got good heads – they are almost ten a penny. It is remarkable to get a bad head on a well-bred dog or bitch now. And I emphasise 'well-bred' dog or bitch. When I was starting, you went for make and shape and as good a head as you could get. People have concentrated too much on heads to the detriment of make and shape.

Those who say that the Bull Terriers in the ring today are not quite as top-class as others in the past, are forgetful. You cannot compare different generations of dogs. They were good in their day, but were they all that much better than those of today? That's a big question. Who knows?'

(Eva Weatherill, from her video *Bully Talk*, 1987)

So what is expected of the Bull Terrier today? What should you look for in a sound animal? The list of requirements for any breed is known as the Breed Standard. These have been updated by the Kennel Club, who claim their ownership. The same format is used for every breed, in an attempt to bring some continuity. The Bull Terrier Standard was altered only a little and alters the dog not at all. It would, however, be useful to consider the Bull Terrier's basic anatomy, and why certain types of conformation are desirable and others harmful. T.J. Horner gives a lucid description of what lies beneath the skin and behind the shape of a Bull Terrier in *All About*

11

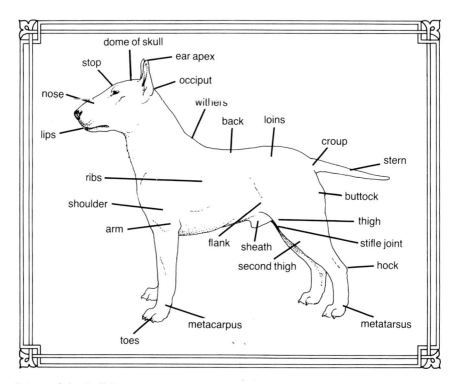

Points of the Bull Terrier.

*the Bull Terrier,* and he has edited an *Illustrated Explanation of the Standard of the Bull Terrier* for the Bull Terrier Club, which clarifies the various statements made in the Breed Standard.

Let us look at some of the traits which you should soon be able to recognise in your own Bull Terrier and in those you see from the ring side.

## The Head

It is generally considered that the Bull Terrier head is egg-shaped, or like the shape of a rugby ball. The head should be in proportion to the rest of the body, have 'downface', 'fillup' and a 'Roman finish'.

The head should have a curved or arc profile when seen from the side, curving from between the ears down to the nose, which should dip down even more. This is known as 'downface'. There may be a slight angle rather than a smooth curve on the brow but this should not be too pronounced. Viewed from the front, the head

12

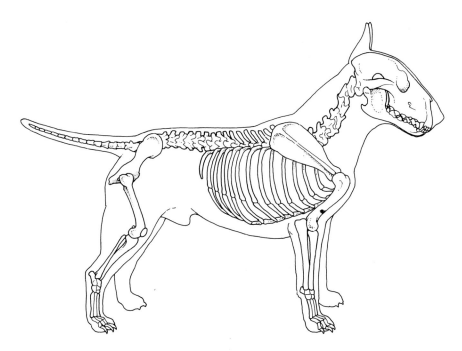

The Bull Terrier skeleton.

should be oval, with a smooth outline along the cheek and side of the face. Between the ears should be flat rather than domed. The face should be filled with bone, giving the head strength and leaving no hollows under the eyes. This is known as 'fillup'. The hollow between the two sinuses in a dog is called 'the stop' and acts as the means by which the forehead is separated from the nasal passages. The angle formed between the cranium and the rest of the face below the stop varies in different breeds, being more noticeable in the downfaced Bull Terrier breed. The absence of stop is a very important show point for the Bull Terrier.

The whole face should be of nearly equal width both at the skull and at the muzzle. The head should be strong but not coarse.

# Eyes

Dogs' eyes are all the same size proportionally – it is the eye opening that varies. There are two main eyelids – an upper and a lower, and a third that lies in the inner corner of the eye flicking over the front of the eye-ball when the eye is touched. The Bull Terrier's eye

The Bull Terrier's eye is
triangular with a dark glint.

opening differs from that of other dogs in that it is triangular, and is
set at an angle, with the corner of the lower eyelid pointing towards
the outer corner of the ear. This is no reflection of the shape of the
eye-ball however, which is roughly spherical, as in any other breed.
The opening is small and the eye is deep-set. In an attack from an
adversary, the surrounding eyelids swell, giving the eye protection
and making it appear to reduce in size. This is one very useful sign
that a silent disagreement between two Bull Terriers is about to
develop into a full-blooded skirmish!

The glint through the slit-like eye-lids of the Bull Terrier is full of
pride. The eyes are most expressive – it only needs the owner to
learn how to read the message being put across. If you offer a
biscuit, he will take it, but the eyes may tell you that he had
something quite different in mind!

For a long time it was thought that dogs had no colour vision, but
recent observations have concluded that while red and green appear
to dogs as neutral, they can distinguish, to a certain degree, between other colours (mainly blue and yellow). They can also differentiate between oval and circular shapes. The colour of the eye

should be black or as dark brown as possible. However, light brown eyes do still appear as do partially blue ones. Occasionally, dark brown or black eyes may have a segment of pigmentation missing from the cornea, making the dog look as though he has a speck of something in his eye. This may colour up as adulthood approaches but often does not. It is stated in the Breed Standard that blue or partially blue eyes are undesirable, but the dog's sight is not impaired by the colour of the iris. Please note that Bull Terriers do not have pink eyes. How often I am asked for 'one of those pink-eyed white dogs'!

# Ears

The Bull Terrier looks at his most intelligent and alert when the ears are placed on top of the head and held stiffly upwards. Those that fan out at an angle of 'ten to two' from the skull look too large and give the dog a clumsy expression. The ears should be upright, the flap having unfolded by about four months old. Whatever the set, it will not impair the hearing; they only act as trumpets, catching the sound waves – the works are 'down below'.

# Mouth

The shape of the muzzle can be seen best in profile. A deep strong square muzzle or a thinner whippety one. A strong under-jaw will give the power needed to grip. However, it should not look as if the under-lip pouts or protrudes as this would indicate that the animal will be undershot when adult. The lips ought to fit neatly. A slack, over-hanging upper lip would be an easy target for a fighting adversary.

There are two parts to the mouth – one known as the vestibule, which is the area between the inside of the lips and cheeks and the teeth, and the other, known as the mouth cavity which takes in the hard and soft palate, the tongue and tissues and the gums and teeth. The teeth can be inspected by raising the upper lip and depressing the lower one at the front. The incisors and canines will then be exposed. By gently opening the mouth and drawing back the lips, the premolars and molars can be examined and counted. The teeth should be a good colour and tartar free, although old dogs

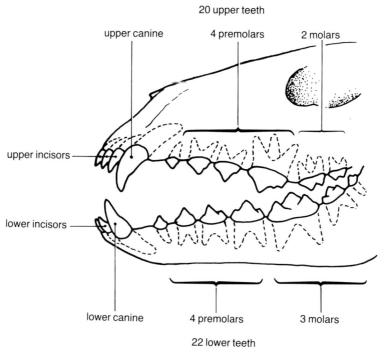

20 upper teeth

upper canine      4 premolars      2 molars

upper incisors

lower incisors

lower canine      4 premolars      3 molars

22 lower teeth

The Bull Terrier jaw.

are bound to have a natural build-up and discoloration. The number of each kind of tooth should be checked along with their alignment and occlusion. There should only be a small inter-dental space between the canine tooth and the first premolar; however, there should be a wide space across the mouth from one canine tooth to the other. This is in contrast to the narrowing cavity that would be present in a finer-muzzled dog. In some puppies a double set of incisor teeth may be present or perhaps fewer than the approved number.

Temporary teeth appear during the first three to four weeks of a dog's life, the two canines arriving first. These are eventually replaced by forty-two permanent teeth at four to five months of age. The adult dog should own:

|  | Incisors | Canines | Premolars | Molars |
|---|---|---|---|---|
| **Upper** | 3 | 1 | 4 | 2 |
| **Lower** | 3 | 1 | 4 | 3 |

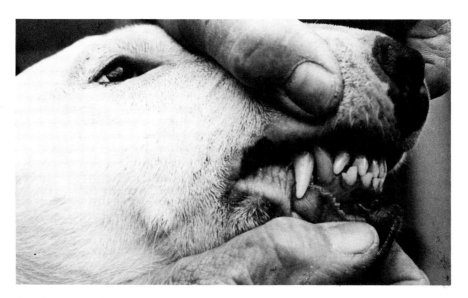

Level or pincer bite.

The lower jaw has three molars compared with two in the upper. The fourth premolar (the Carnassial tooth) in the upper set is paired with and looks similar to the first molar in the lower set. The first to third premolars are changed at between five and six months of age, the small first premolar sometimes not appearing until later. It is at about this time that the upper first molar appears, followed by the second molar in the lower jaw between six and eight months. The upper second molar is frequently absent altogether. Some of the premolars (usually those immediately behind the canine tooth), can be missing too and although not considered a serious fault, dogs lacking the required number of teeth may be faulted in the show-ring.

In a pincer level mouth the teeth fit on top of each other – the dog can nip. The scissor bite cuts as would a pair of scissors and is the prefered mouth – the small front top teeth (the upper incisors), fitting in front of the lower incisors.

## Undershot

Undershot is a term used to describe a dog's mouth when the teeth or under-jaw protrude beyond the upper teeth and jaw. For owners who have not taken a particular interest in the teeth placement, the first indication that their puppy has become undershot is when everything ripped or chewed has a very jagged edge.

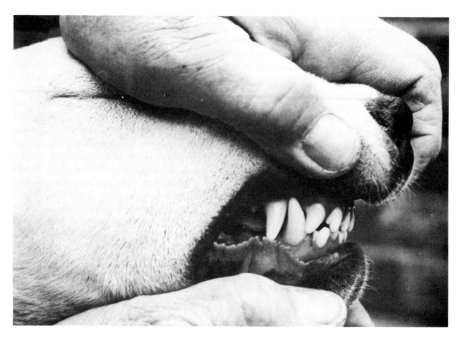

Correct scissor bite from the side.

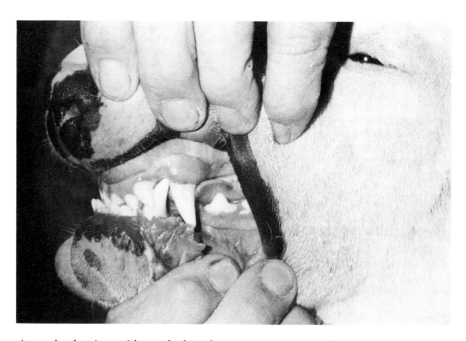

An undershot jaw with crooked teeth.

18

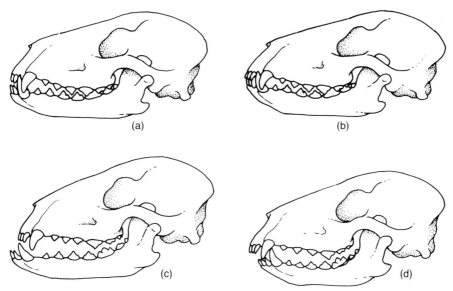

(a) Level or pincer bite, (b) correct scissor bite,
(c) undershot jaw and (d) overshot jaw.

## Overshot

Overshot describes the upper jaw when it protrudes severely over
and beyond the lower jaw.

# Nose

The Bull Terrier's nose should be black, whatever the colour of the
dog. It should also dip a little giving his profile a 'Roman finish'.
White Bull Terriers may be lacking in the necessary pigmentation
and carry black spots on a pink nose or the nose may be only
partially coloured. Butterfly noses – coloured to resemble a butterfly
– are not acceptable, nor are pink noses or 'dudley' noses. Most
puppies are born with pink noses which begin to gain colour at two
to three weeks – tiny grey dots gradually darken and join up to form
black. Sometimes the colouring spreads beyond the nose to the
surrounding skin. Other pups' noses do not colour until eight to ten
weeks of age. It is interesting to note that in certain countries nose-
prints are taken in a similar manner to the taking of finger prints,
and are used for identification of the dog.

# Neck

The head should be carried well on a long, tense, firmly muscled neck widening from head to shoulders. Although arched, the neck should not be long and thin like that of a sheep. The handler who strings up his Bull Terrier when moving him in the ring will end up with a dog with a neck taking on this characteristic. A Bull Terrier should be moved on a slack leash to show off the length and carriage of the neck. The neck should have a 'solid' feel to it without looking gross. The length of each of the seven vertebrae contained in it determines the overall length of the neck. The apparent length of the neck depends mainly on the placing of the scapula (shoulder blade) – whether it is sloping back at its upper end, or more upright, which appears to both shorten the neck and influence the angle at which the neck and head are carried.

# Shoulder

In order to determine the placement of the shoulder blade, place one finger at the centre of the upper edge and using the other hand

The shoulder blade and upper arm of the Bull Terrier.

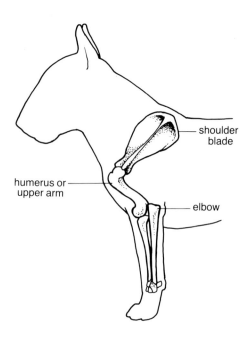

shoulder blade

humerus or upper arm

elbow

place one finger on the shoulder joint at the lower end. The angle of the line joining these two points and the horizontal ground line upon which the dog is standing will give you an angle of forty-five degrees or less for a good shoulder placement. An angle of sixty to seventy degrees would indicate an upright shoulder. The angle of the shoulder blade also depends upon the degree of curvature of the ribs which can force the upper edges of the two shoulder blades further apart and into an upright position. If three fingers can be placed between the upper edges of the two shoulder blades it would indicate an upright shoulder, though Bull Terriers have a greater width here than most other breeds.

The length of stride is determined by the angle between the shoulder blade and the upper arm. If this is too steep the stride is shortened, and short mincing steps are seen. A well laid shoulder will give a good angle and reach of stride.

# Elbow

The length of the humerus (the bone from the shoulder blade to the elbow), determines the position of the elbow as being well back and tucked into the sides of the body. The elbow should come directly below the top of the shoulder blade, or it will be forward on the chest. 'Out-at-elbows' is the term used to describe elbows which stand out from the chest; this can be caused by upright shoulders and short upper arms with bulging muscles.

# Back

A strong back with a slightly arched loin is necessary to support the workings within the abdomen. The top line should be level. The Bull Terrier should not be flat sided or of equal depth along the whole of his side.

# Ribs

The ribs ought to be well sprung or rounded to allow for the expansion of the lungs within, with strong muscle, and considerable depth – down as far as the elbow and curving up to the belly.

21

# Legs

The legs should be in proportion to the overall size of the dog. The whole dog should look 'square'. As a rough guide, the forelegs should be the same length as the distance between fore and hind legs. The hocks, which should be short, contain seven bones. If they turn in they are known as 'cow-hocks', and give a knitting action when moving.

When viewed from the front the chest should be broad, forelegs straight, elbows tight and hind legs parallel to the front ones.

# Feet

Bull Terriers should have small but thick feet, the hind pair being finer than the fore. The toes should be well arched rather than flat. With long strides straight from the shoulder, the foot lands on the two centre nails and then takes the weight on the thick hind triangular pad.

# Hindquarters

The propulsion or driving force comes from the hindquarters. These need to be well muscled with good angulation – the stifle joint and the hock must be well bent. Unlike those dogs bred with increased angulation, the Bull Terrier breed does not suffer from hip displacia. This places the dog's feet behind his body instead of beneath it, changing the direction of the thrust into the hip joint and lessening the amount of muscle that surrounds it. Luxating patella, or slipping kneecap can, however, cause trouble for Bull Terriers. The patella is small and held mostly within muscle, gliding up and down the groove of the trochlea, the function of which is to keep the two bones correctly aligned. When the patella slips, the stifle swings outwards.

# Tail

The tail should be low and carried horizontally, unless the dog is excited or angry. A flag-pole of a tail, set high or a tail curling over

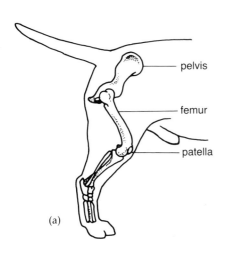

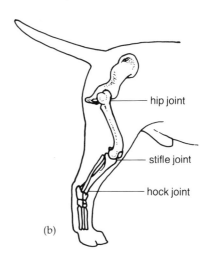

(a) Strong and (b) weak hindquarters.

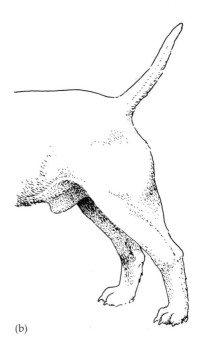

(a) Correct tail carriage and (b) high-set tail.

towards the back of the dog, look off-balance and might indicate straight stifles.

# Coat

A Bull Terrier's coat is made up of strong short hairs which manage to stick into clothing by their fine tapering ends. They can be extremely difficult to remove! The whole coat should lie smoothly over tightly fitting skin, so that the dog does not have ridges of loose flesh which could be a target for an adversary. Growing puppies appear to have 'skin growing weeks' and they will have a short period when their skin seems far too big for them, but this is only in readiness for the adult frame which will catch up and fill out all the wrinkles. There is an undercoat present in the winter which is of a softer texture. Occasionally, bunches of coloured hair, ranging from five to fifty hairs, appear in the undercoat. These are known as 'ticks'. They usually disappear again when the undercoat is shed for summer. These will be of whichever colour the Bull Terrier is carrying, and are often only present in the puppy undercoat.

# Colour

The white Bull Terrier should have a pure white coat, though markings above the collar, such as behind the ears or elsewhere on the head are permissible. Any markings elsewhere are known as mismarks and are frowned upon in the show-ring. The white dog is in fact a coloured animal in which the colour has been subjected to an inhibiting factor. Grey markings on the pink skin of a white Bull Terrier – skin pigmentation – may show through the coat when the undercoat is not present or when the dog is wet, but this should not be penalised. The coloured Bull Terriers can be seen as brindle, black brindle, red, fawn and tricolour, but brindle is dominant and therefore is prefered. Usually the coloured Bull Terriers have a white blaze on the head, white chest, white underbelly, white socks and a white tip to their tail. Those that are all coloured are known as 'solids' and if mated will only breed coloureds, even if their partner is white. A coloured should have more colour than white visible – the colour must predominate.

In some countries white and coloured Bull Terriers are shown separately in the ring but are judged to the same Standard – after all some of them will be litter brothers and sisters.

# Movement

A Bull Terrier that has good conformation does not necessarily prove to be a good mover, even when the neck, shoulders, fore and hindquarters are all that might be desired. The dog's centre of gravity varies from one breed to another according to the relative weights of the front and hind portions of the body. The body has to travel parallel to the ground wherever its weight distribution may be. The relationship between the two portions of the body and the ease of movement go to make up the dog's 'balance'. This depends on the front and back portions of the body working in synchronisation. The movement depends on the particular gait and the acquired momentum. At a fast walk the forefoot may be lifted from the ground before the hind foot has reached it, and only two feet are on the ground where there would usually be three. This is when the Bull Terrier tends to roll towards the side with the least support. At a trot only two feet ought to be touching the ground at one time. When the dog is trotting, the front and back legs should be parallel to each other. Some develop the habit of 'pacing' – the hind and fore limbs of each side advance together and the Bull Terrier displays a sailor's gait. This is ugly and cannot be performed at a high speed. Many bitches develop this style of walking when carrying a litter, and retain it long after the need for such an inhibiting style of motion has passed. A good mover will reach out with the forelegs and have great thrust and drive from the hindquarters. The pads of both the fore and hind feet should be visible from behind – an indication that the hocks and knees are being flexed correctly. Length of stride, thrust and balance can be determined by viewing the dog from the side.

Conformation alone is not enough however – characteristics and temperament are also of great importance.

# Temperament and Characteristics

Once you come to know a Bull Terrier, you will never want another breed. Bull Terriers are a breed apart from all others and if you fall victim to their charm, no other dog will have the same hold over you. A Bull Terrier should be good-natured, friendly, patient, outgoing and adaptable and completely loyal. They are extremely affectionate to their own family and are renowned for their care of children and the elderly. They can be mischievous and act the clown, are quick to know if a person is afraid of them and will delight in taking advantage, yet they are amenable to discipline.

Although even two centuries ago it was recognised that Bull Terriers were often devotedly loyal to their masters, it must be remembered that these animals were bred for the fighting pits, to bait and to kill other animals, and these instincts can still be there. Today, aggressiveness towards another dog, though frowned upon, may be understandable but any towards people is not to be tolerated. Breeders of repute can select good-tempered breed lines and make sure that in aiming to improve other aspects of their particular line they do not double up on bad-tempered ancestry. Owners and environment usually influence the hereditary traits that are more apparent in their Bull Terrier by their handling and development training during and after puppyhood. Bull Terriers are enthusiastic, energetic and exhausting if they have not been trained as puppies. They require a great deal of attention in their formative months and must not be allowed to become pack leaders. This can take many

Bull Terriers are 'of a sweet disposition and amenable to discipline'.

forms – they may become bossy, possessive or jealous; they may bark in a demanding tone or insist on standing on top of their owner when sitting – all to be the dominant member of the pack. This type of behaviour should not be encouraged. To sit beside their owner's feet or to be rolled over on their backs to have their tummies tickled is a position of submission that instills into the puppy his place in the pecking order of the family. Hours of attention in the form of playing, outings, grooming and affection tempered with firm discipline will result in a well developed character of even temperament.

Bull Terriers are seldom scared and never terrified which is why they can be depended upon to be reliable with children. They will not mistake an accidental blow for a deliberate hit. They may appear to be obstinate, but they are not unintelligent. Handling them is very similar to dealing with a stubborn child, except that should you decide to set your wit against theirs, they will win! Bull Terriers, as any other dogs, are quick to reflect the fear of their owners and in an unknown situation a nervous dog will grow confident when he realises that no one else is worried. Traffic noise to the country dog, a flight of steps to the flat-dweller or the sound of the sea and the vastness of the water on that first visit to the coast are all new experiences that can be taken in their stride with the help of sensible owners.

Everyone who has owned more than one Bull Terrier knows how their personalities differ from each other, yet there are particular tricks and habits which must be peculiar to the inheritance of the Bull Terrier. Of course, the many general canine characteristics are also present in the Bull Terrier – those that forbid an adult dog or bitch to harm a puppy, the animal language when one dog meets another, boundary rights, dominance of, and subservience to, the pack-leader and members of the pack.

# 2

# The Bull Terrier Puppy

Having decided that you want a Bull Terrier in preference to any other breed of dog, the next task is to discover from where to obtain one. You will be expected to pay a considerable sum of money for this new acquisition to the household. You will want quality for money, but a dog should never be considered merely as a new commodity for the home – the returns you will gain in terms of devotion and companionship are beyond price. Firstly, there are places that you should not consider – pet shops, puppy farms and market stalls. It is no good feeling sorry for the poor mite sitting shivering in the corner of a pen, or even the more boisterous soul romping around, pulling at your heart-strings with their appealing eyes. Back-street breeders are not even cheaper – far from it. They demand the current price without having put any of the care and nourishment of the devoted breeder into the rearing of their pups. They also probably went to the nearest Bull Terrier dog to mate their bitch, regardless of temperament or faults.

You may decide that you wish to devote yourself to the rearing of a puppy that has had a poor start in life, and are prepared to take on all the problems that come from inconsiderate and uninformed breeding by those who do not care who buys their puppies and who willingly allow a litter to be sold through another agency. Certainly if you see such puppies you will want to buy one of them, if only because you know you can offer them a quality of life that they may not otherwise find. We have had three such come our way over the years, known fondly as the 'passengers' in the kennel. The youngest, now eight years old, is at this moment upstairs on my bed; our lives have been undoubtedly enriched by their company.

However, if you are looking for a foundation Bull Terrier that will be a loved companion for the entire family and possibly the start to the interesting hobby of showing and breeding dogs, you require a quality animal of sound temperament. You therefore need to know something of its breeding and the breeder. The best informed source would be The Bull Terrier Club for your area. In Great Britain there are The Bull Terrier Club and ten regional Bull Terrier Clubs. America has The Bull Terrier Club of America and clubs in various States. The telephone number of the Honorary Secretary of any of these clubs can be obtained from the Kennel Club of Great Britain in London or the American Kennel Club. They will give you information regarding your nearest club. The honorary secretaries will be able to suggest reliable breeders in your area and they will also tell you the date and venue of any shows that may be held in the near future – for this is the next place to look for your breeder.

Bull Terrier Club shows are for Bull Terriers only and if you go along you will be made most welcome, meet other owners, breeders and enthusiasts, and most important of all, you will see Bull Terriers. Here you can see youngsters of six months to a year old as well as the adults. Seeing adults, dogs and bitches, will help you to make sure that you still want this particular breed. It is also helpful to see the whites and coloureds (brindle, tricolour, red or fawn), together. Ask any Committee Member and they will put you in touch with a breeder there who may be able to help you find a puppy, that fits your requirements regarding sex and colour. Alternatively, you should obtain the canine newspapers – *Dog World, Our Dogs, Kennel Gazette, American Kennel Gazette* or *Purebred Dogs*. The advertisements in these usually name the kennel, the sire and dam of the litter and any other relevant information. Sometimes the local newspaper will have an advertisement for puppies for sale. These are usually from a bitch who is a family pet having one litter. They are often carefully bred and have had every attention lavished upon them by devoted owners. Information about the pedigree should be obtained and checked – the stud dog owner could confirm the details for you. It is certainly comforting to have your first Bull Terrier from a local source in that you can contact the breeder if you want information about any particular detail as your Bull Terrier matures. We have puppies back to see us whenever their owners are travelling in our direction.

During the preliminary arrangements with the breeder, explain exactly what sort of dog you want and your household circumstances as regard to housing the puppy and whether or not somebody is always at home. Bull Terriers can vary in their characteristics even within the same litter, just as two children in the same family may differ. If possible, arrange to see the sire and the dam and any other relations of your prospective puppy that might be at the kennels. Make a definite appointment to visit the breeder so that sufficient time is allocated in the daily routine to be able to answer all your queries and show you the litter. Should you be unable to keep the appointment it is only courteous to phone and cancel or rearrange the appointment – breeders have very full schedules and do not want to waste time waiting for people when they could be walking their dogs. If the travelling distance is too far to be able to make the preliminary visit, then several long telephone calls will have to be made, and do be prepared for the breeder to arrange for another Club member who resides in your vicinity to visit you. The sensible, caring buyer is only too happy to meet another Bull Terrier fancier who can help with any small queries, and the breeder's mind will be at rest that the puppy that has been reared so carefully, will continue to be cared for in a similar manner.

Take someone with you when you visit the puppies for the first time. Either someone who has bred Bull Terrier puppies or at least seen several litters of this age, or else someone who is not interested in the breed but has an affinity with dogs. Whereas you may be bowled over at the sight of bouncy friendly pups, your less sentimental companion will be astute enough to advise you, if they feel the whole set-up is wrong, to go home and consider the situation. Whether you are the buyer or the breeder, an excellent maxim is to follow your instincts. Never sell to somebody you have any doubts about. You will invariably be right. They will be dealers, passing the pup on to an unknown buyer, or else the uncaring type of owner who really only wants a Bull Terrier for the image, and when it proves to be too much trouble it will be back on your doorstep – if it's lucky – or else passed on to one home after another. It is far better to keep the pup until the right people come along.

When the time comes to choose a puppy, select a happy inquisitive one in preference to the quiet one who backs off or sits in a corner. He may have the best conformation of all the litter and if that is what you are after, don't neglect him. He may only behave in this way because he is feeling tired, but it is generally considered that a shy, nervous puppy may be slow to mix with the family, may not have the right disposition for the show-ring or may end up as an aggressive adult.

Look for a lively, plump pup, not too long in the back, with strong bones and a sturdy rear-end with well-bent stifle joints. Whippity straight-legged back-ends with long tails will probably always re-

where he can feel secure is the aim and it must not appear as a punishment. Once the house-cage has been established, short journeys sitting in the cage in the car should follow. These should take the form of an exciting outing to help instil in his mind a pleasurable feeling attached to car journeys in a cage. The cage must be large enough for him to be able to stand, turn around and lie down in, and if lined with warm bedding he will have a far more comfortable ride than if sitting on wobbly knees or trampling from one seat to another and from the front to the back of the car. Passengers and driver too will arrive at their destination tidy and calm and ready to enjoy the company of their Bull Terrier.

# Grooming

Your Bull Terrier puppy will have been kept clean by his mother or by the breeder for the first few weeks of his life. His face and rear parts will need to be kept clean daily. Using cotton wool dampened with warm water is usually quite sufficient. Any stubborn mark such as oil or tar should be removed with a little baby shampoo. Whenever the puppy has muddy feet take the opportunity of dipping them in a bowl of lukewarm water as this is the easiest way to clean them and will prepare him for having his feet attended to without alarming him. I put my puppies into the sink with an inch of water to wash their feet. This way they become used to the sink for when they have to have a bath. When too big for this, they progress to the big bath and shower without trouble.

Training to stand on a table for grooming is also best carried out while he is small and easy to lift. It is much easier if the dog is at your hand height where there is a good light than if you have to attend to him on the floor. Ears, eyes and nails can easily be checked, and a light brushing using a soft cloth or soft-bristled brush to make his coat shine, should be given. All this attention while standing on the table teaches him not to be afraid when he has to be lifted on to the table at the vet's. Of course you will not be lifting him up and down every day when he is an adult, but he will have learnt by then that to stand still on the table is the desired mode of practice.

# Training

The puppy will love to explore and romp in the garden accompanied by his new and trusted pack-leader. Soon he will be running in and out of doors confidently, each bush and flower becoming part of imaginary games rather than a frightening adversary. Then is the time for basic training and an introduction to a collar and lead.

## 'Come'

Once a name has been established amongst the family – one that rolls easily off the tongue when repeated continuously – then use it on every possible occasion so that the puppy comes to recognise it as being something to do with him. Next comes the stage of trying to get him to come to you when called. The earlier this is taught the better, for his own safety. I use puppies' liking for their daily dose of malt extract. They are already familiar with their daily enjoyment of licking the malt off a spoon. By standing at the door, when they are playing in the garden, holding a large jar of malt and the spoons and calling in a high-pitched happy voice, they will stop what they are doing and come rushing down to be the first to get the treat. (Take care, if doing this, not to let them bite the spoon.) When the puppies go to their new home all that has to be added to this trick is the use of their name. Use something that appeals to their stomachs and that they will recognise from afar, call their name in such an exciting manner that what you are offering is bound to sound better than their present activity and then praise and reward liberally when they respond. This needs to be repeated several times a day if you want to reinforce the lesson. (If you should use the malt extract as your bait, remember to give only a little on the teaspoon as the daily dose is only one teaspoon and if exceeded a puppy may get diarrhoea.)

## 'Sit'

This is another easy command to teach. Wait until the puppy is sitting and then praise him using the word 'sit'. It sounds simple, and it is. Reinforce your praise with food and before you know where you are, if he thinks you have food you will find him sitting as a means of asking you for some! Later you will be able to train him to sit instantly you give the command – patience is the key

SOCIALISATION

word. Do not get cross with him. If you find yourself getting
annoyed, leave any training for a while and come back later on
when you are feeling fresh.

## Collar

Most breeders will have taught the puppy to accept his collar. This
is more easily done when the bitch is with them as she will inspect
the collar and give the pup a good wash to explain that all is well.
However, he will not have worn it continuously as it can be
dangerous for romping puppies. One may catch a claw in another's
collar, or they may play games of tugging at each other's collar
which is not to be encouraged. Now he is going to be expected to
wear a collar full-time and have a dangling name disc which will
annoy him. The collar should be of the ribbed nylon type – narrow
and lightweight for a puppy's first collar. This can be changed for a
stronger one when he is older. Bull Terriers have a knack of making
their necks thick and fat when having a collar fitted and then
suddenly long and thin so that the collar slips off over their heads as
soon as any pressure is put to bear on it. For this reason I prefer to
use the type of collar that is self adjusting by means of a short chain
of the martingale type. All my dogs have these in various widths as
house collars.

Your puppy should have his collar put on immediately before
eating so that he has something other to think about than the
constraint around his neck. Another opportunity is when nursing
the puppy on your lap so that he is comfortable and secure and will
hardly notice the collar. In both cases the collar should only be left
on for a short while and certainly not once he has settled down for
sleep, as it is then that he will have time to become aware of it, try
scratching to remove it and may catch a claw in it. Gradually the
collar can be left on for longer periods until the puppy is no longer
aware of it and it can become a permanent fixture.

## Lead

Use a nylon slip lead such as those worn in the show-ring at first.
Slip it on when he is very busy playing with you in the garden and
make absolutely sure that it does not pull taut. It should provide just
enough restraint around his neck for him to realise that something is
controlling him. The game will continue and his desire to follow you

47

will encourage him to go where the lead dictates. If opposition ensues, do not be tempted to force your will over him as it would only mean that, on a slip lead, you would strangle him. Rather let it hang loosely on his shoulders while you distract him. Each lead training session should not be any longer than five or six minutes at first. An alternative is for a lightweight lead with a very light clip to be clasped to the collar (once he is used to it) and then left on the floor so that while playing it drags around with him. This however needs constant supervision to ensure that the lead does not become entangled with shrubs or, if indoors, with chair-legs and cause an accident, or that the puppy does not decide that leads should be carried around in the mouth or chewed.

Once he is accustomed to the basic idea, then very gently persuade the puppy that it would be extremely interesting to walk in the direction you wish him to go – around the garden path, or down to the gate. Remember not to let him walk where other dogs (apart from those of your own household), may have been, as he does not have the necessary protection from his inoculations yet. He will already be used to you carrying him to these various locations, so carry him to some exciting place, a few yards from your door, put him down on the ground and after exploring the area, attempt to walk the return route. He will soon realise that the safety of home is quickly reached and his more adventurous spirit will take over – he will be prepared to walk away from the house towards the garden gate of his own free will. Keep pace with him so that the lead is always slack. Do not let him think that pulling on the lead is desirable – remember he could eventually weigh eighty pounds (thirty-six kilograms)! Continue to make everything a game for the puppy and should he show a tendency to follow, encourage it. Spaniels, for example, naturally follow to heel around the house. To Bull Terriers it is not a natural custom, but if the puppy has decided that you are the pack-leader, or has adopted you as his replacement mother, then encourage the situation. Walking to heel will be that much easier to teach.

By the time the Bull Terrier's course of injections is completed he will be between three-and-a-half and four-and-a-half months old and should be fully prepared to venture forth into the world beyond the garden gate. You may however have bought an older puppy – the breeder may have decided to keep the litter until the course of vaccinations was completed, or maybe you have a puppy that has been 'run on' by the breeder in the hope that the 'show potential' of his breeding is developing into a 'possible show-dog'. This pup may come into your home, fully acclimatised, lead-trained, house-trained and so forth, but it is sometimes the case that they have been left to their own devices for long periods in a kennel and run, and new owners will have to start from the beginning.

By the very requirements of their activity the majority of breeders live in the country and the puppies are used to country sounds and smells. These pups are often the ones that become shy, nervous and eventually aggressive. The stress of coming into a normal environ-ment takes many weeks to overcome. Just because a puppy is fully inoculated does not mean it is all right to plunge him straight into the ordeal of walking through city streets, the smell of car fumes, dust and a cacophony of sound. It may take weeks to build up confidence. Breeders may say that some breeds should not be trained for the show-ring or for Obedience Trials until they are over twelve months old, but that does not mean that they can miss their general socialisation.

# 4

# Training an Adolescent Dog

Your young Bull Terrier is to be your companion and friend, and therefore a well-mannered lady or gentleman is preferable to a boisterous hooligan with over-possessive tendencies. It is up to you to encourage your friend along a better course of training to become an acceptable animal in society.

Every Bull Terrier needs to be a member of the family – not chained up or left in a kennel all day long. He is a very active animal, always busy, and likes to be at the centre of the family activity. Whether the family consists of young children or of an elderly couple who can give the dog their undivided attention, he will do his best to please, provided he has been shown what is required of him.

By the time your Bull Terrier is six months old he should know how to walk on a lead, be house-trained, and generally know how to behave. By now the family bond should be building up, he should have come to trust his pack-leader and you should be able to have faith in him. Regular but brief training sessions every day will help to build up this bond, as will grooming sessions.

## Grooming

Grooming the coat helps to remove dust and mud and any loose hair. Even white coats shine with health when regularly brushed or rubbed down with a soft cloth. Grooming also provides an opportunity to check nails, ears, eyes and teeth and so deal with any problems as soon as they appear, before it becomes necessary to go to a veterinary surgeon. Nails may need filing, though with regular road work they are usually kept short naturally. Ears should be kept clean with a proprietary cleansing solution available from pet shops. They should not be poked or prodded. Once the cleansing solution has softened any build-up of wax, a gentle wipe-out with cotton buds can clear the outer ear quite painlessly. Eyes ought to be rinsed with cotton wool soaked in warm water to remove dust or grit if the dog has been exercised in dusty areas or through meadow grass. Teeth can be cleaned using ordinary toothpaste on a piece of towelling and rubbed on each tooth. Most dogs enjoy the taste and soon learn to allow this procedure. If his breath is very unpleasant check the diet. Is he having sufficient hard tack to keep his teeth clean, and his stomach in order? Has he been wormed recently? After early puppy worming he should be wormed at four and six months and then every six months or according to veterinary advice if he is having the worming injections.

## Ears

Puppies' ears gradually come up on to the top of their heads. After unfolding from ten days onwards, they seem to come up sideways and at about eight weeks old have started to bring up the flap to form an upright trumpet. These flaps bouncing up and down give the puppies that cute bouncy appearance but they should gradually become stronger and more upright and be well on their way by three months old. Once the puppy starts changing his teeth they may flop down again, but if they were up beforehand they will usually return once the teething period is over. If the ear-flaps are particularly heavy they may be too much for the blood vessels to hold upright and as the dog gets older and bigger this problem will increase. Between four and six months he may need help. Consult the breeder of the puppy first as he will know from experience with the pup's parents whether heavy ears are a tendency or whether they have come up eventually.

The best way you can help your puppy, after having massaged the ears daily when giving him his cuddle, is to tape them up. He may look as though he has a pair of rugby posts on top of his head for a couple of weeks, but if it is going to help him to get his ears where they should be, why worry any more than you would if he had a splint on a broken limb? To tape the ears:

1 Clean the inside of the ear and make sure it is dry.
2 Fold the ear in half lengthwise so that it is in a long cone shape.
3 Bind it round with a strip of medicinal adhesive plaster.
4 Repeat with the other ear.
5 With more medicinal adhesive plaster, wrap one turn around

At five months, the ears may be too heavy and drop down. In such cases, they should be taped up until they are stronger.

Once the ears have gained in strength, they will stay erect, even when the tape is removed.

    an ear and across (but not touching) the top of the dog's head, and wrap round the other ear returning across the bridge to cover the exposed sticky part of the strip.

6 Leave on for five days and when removed the ears will be upright though they may gradually flop down after a short while. In a show dog the tape can be removed just before entering the ring and the ears will probably remain upright long enough to finish the class. You may need to repeat the taping but check first to see if the ears look sore from sweating inside. If this is the case then leave alone for a few days. The tape should be removed using surgical spirit, otherwise the dog's hair may come away as well! It usually takes about two weeks of this treatment to give the blood vessels a chance to strengthen sufficiently to hold the ears upright without assistance.

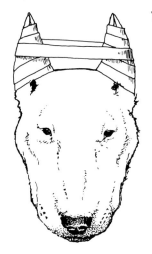

Taped ears.

# Commands

There are certain instructions that a Bull Terrier should learn to obey instantly for his own safety and for your control of his actions. The most urgent of these is for him to understand that 'No' means 'No'. When caught in the act of some misdemeanour a clear disapproving note in your voice will give him the general idea and if this is not sufficient a firm tap on his rear will make him understand! This is only worth doing at the time when the error is being committed. It is no good taking the pup indoors and then smacking him. He will not have the slightest idea that the smack is connected with his behaviour earlier. Rather he will associate it with something that has happened within the last two minutes, since coming indoors. As soon as he has realised his mistake, change your tactics, find some reason to call him to you, praise him and play with him. Punishment must be meted out at the time of the crime and when the pup is within reach. Do not on any account chase him as you will end up circling the kitchen table with the dog under the impression that it is a good game. If you call the Bull Terrier to you do not then chastise him. He will associate the punishment with his latest action – that of coming to you when called. This should receive a reward not punishment.

'Come', 'Sit' and 'No' are commands that can be taught in the first weeks that the puppy is in his new home. It is far easier to persuade the small dog that you mean what you say at this stage. At six months you may have a battle of wills on your hands. Always remember that a Bull Terrier is extremely obstinate and needs the same tactics as those used when dealing with a stubborn child. Do not try to set your will against his – he will win! You will both end up irritable and nothing constructive will have been accomplished. If this happens abandon the attempt and try again later when you are both calmer.

## 'Come'

The same tactics should be used as for the younger puppy – Bull Terriers think with their stomachs! On calling two teenage dogs to come, one owner watched as both dogs shot straight up some cliffs to fields where they could find themselves amongst farm animals. He sat down on the beach, held up an imaginary tube of sweets and yelled out 'Polos!' – two white tornadoes returned down the cliffs at full tilt! He admits that even he was suprised that the trick worked. If caught in the desperate situation where the dog thinks you are playing a chasing game when you try to catch him, and will not come on command, turn and run in the opposite direction, he will very quickly realise that the game is not of his making any more and will follow you instead.

## 'Sit'

Puppies that have learnt this command know what it means and will sit quite readily, but immediately leap up again. Only when he thinks it is a way of asking for food does he remain sitting for more than a few seconds. He now needs to learn to remain sitting until the signal to move off is given. Persevere at every given opportunity.

He should sit whenever he is to have his lead put on and remain until you are ready to set forth on the walk. Once clipped on, drop the rest of the lead on the floor and put your foot on it so that he cannot get up. Make him remain at 'sit' for the few moments that it takes for you to sort out your keys and be ready to leave. The next opportunity will come as soon as you are outside the door and need to check that the door is properly closed and locked. When you reach the first curb make him sit again, and at every curb after that throughout the walk. There is little need to worry about your white

'Sit.'

Bull Terrier getting his hindquarters muddy on a wet day, you will soon notice that he does not sit down heavily at these roadside halts. Rather, he crouches with his weight distributed between his hind legs and his tail. As little as possible is actually touching the ground.

He will soon realise that these halts are temporarily necessary if he wishes to continue his walk. Do not proceed until he is sitting and you have been able to slacken any tension on the lead. Only then give him a command such as 'walk', to indicate that you are now going to cross the road at a brisk pace and in a straight ahead direction. Do not meander diagonally across any road, however quiet. Indoors, the command 'sit' can be given whenever you know you are in a position to enforce its observance and then reward an instant response.

Next, the command should be issued when the dog is too far away for you to be able to forcibly press his hindquarters down to the sit position. Make it a game in the garden, or on the end of a flexi-lead. It takes time, but it is essential. One Bull Terrier in London was prevented from running on to a dual carriageway and causing an accident as well as her own certain death when, having broken her collar, panicked, and raced away from her owner, she dropped into the sit position on his command.

## 'Stay'

This seems to be a command that Bull Terriers prefer to ignore! In the house, he will continue to sit until it looks as though there may be some doubt as to whether you intend to reward him – he is not actually obeying any command to stay. Outside, particularly at a distance, if given the command to 'sit' followed by the command 'stay', he may do so for a few moments, but then tend to get up and wander casually to the nearest interesting sniff and feign an intense interest until you have arrived on the scene. Training to stay at any distance really needs two people so that one can go ahead and if the Bull Terrier stands up, he will run straight into the helper who can return him to the 'sit and stay' position.

## 'Heel'

Keeping your Bull Terrier on your left, he should learn to make left-hand and right-hand turns and to turn about.

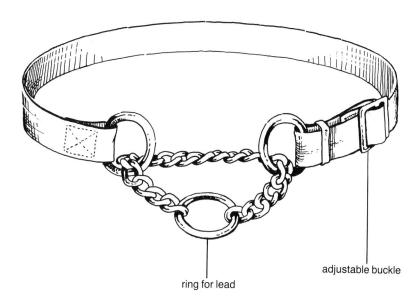

ring for lead

adjustable buckle

Outdoor collar.

# Collar and Lead

Now that your Bull Terrier is stronger, more wilful and prefers to follow his own private pursuits than to pay attention to you, a strong collar and lead are advisable. Ribbed nylon collars are all right for indoors, but a sensible leather collar with a strong buckle should be worn when outside. Avoid very wide collars, as these merely shorten the look of the length of neck and make your dog look coarse. A studded collar should be avoided too, as Bull Terriers will push past anybody or anything that is in their way, and the studs will snag clothes, ladder tights and scratch bare legs.

A choke chain is very useful for training purposes, but it must be the large link variety as those made from fine links catch the dog's hair and pull it out. You should never need to use a pinch or spike collar – the kind with spikes that stick into the dog when the collar is jerked. This is not the way to train a Bull Terrier. These types of collar are not permitted in the show-ring. The choke chain must be put on the correct way round. It should be on in such a manner that the lead is attached to the ring at the end that has come over the top of the dog's neck, leaving the ring at the end of the chain that has come under the neck free to fall loose when the lead is slackened. This way you can jerk the lead to obtain the dog's attention and immediately slacken when the collar too will slacken.

57

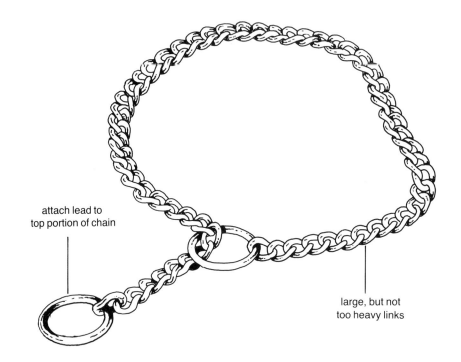

attach lead to
top portion of chain

large, but not
too heavy links

Choke chain.

A six-foot lead is ideal for training your Bull Terrier as it provides enough length for him to be free and recalled. With the dog on your left side the lead should be grasped at a convenient height for your left hand but as close to the collar as possible. The end of the lead should be clasped in, not wound round, your right hand, so that it can be fed out through your left hand when the dog moves further away from you. With the dog on your left, start with your left foot, and walk at a brisk speed. If he pulls away give a jerk on the chain and return him to the correct position. Always use his name before giving any command and use the same commands. As soon as the choke chain has been jerked it must be released again, so that it is the noise of the chain together with the jerk that draws the dog's attention back to the task in hand. If he is allowed to pull continually on the choke chain it merely becomes a contest, with you being towed along. Unless you are able to keep up with the dog you will not be able to slacken the lead and he will come to think that you wish to be propelled on your walks in this manner. Break this up by practising some turns and reverse directions until he has forgotten about pulling. Bull Terriers are prone to adding their own interpretation to everything they are being taught and most of my Bull Terriers get the idea that my heel is about three feet in front of my toes, particularly the dogs who always have to be the leader if they can possibly get away with it!

Training should be fun. If the dog is frightened he will not learn. Dogs learn by association and must feel happy and confident, receiving praise continually. Give him opportunities to be in the right and therefore deserving of praise. A few minutes training every day can become a happy time for your Bull Terrier to look forward to, a time when you are doing some activity together, but it will only be effective if it is short and regular. A lesson which drags on and on one day and then no lesson for days will be of little value.

Possessiveness is a problem that can cause confrontations between you and your Bull Terrier. It is by far the best policy to ensure that confrontation does not occur. Give the dog his meal and leave him in peace to eat it. Why should you have to interfere with his dish in the middle of his supper? If he has been given a bone then leave him in his kennel or bed to enjoy it. This way you will avoid a tussle of wills. Bear in mind that you too would be possessive if removal of your dinner-plate was threatened!

There will be times in his life when you will need to chastise your Bull Terrier. As a puppy, a folded newspaper is sufficient. It is the noise that he does not like, and eventually you will find that to bang the newspaper against your leg is enough to warn him to behave. Punishment should be a short sharp smack on the hindquarters, never on the head or face, and only when the crime is committed *never* later, as the animal will not have the slightest idea what it was for, and will end up associating it with something else. Similarly, never continue the punishment, such as by leaving him shut outside, or continuing to sound cross for the rest of the morning, as he will end up bewildered and sullen. *Never* hit out in a fit of temper, even if it is your most valued article that has been ruined. Why did you leave it where he could reach it?

As he reaches adulthood your dog should be quite capable of understanding right from wrong purely from the tone of your voice. Dogs are often punished to relieve their owner's own feelings of guilt. It is very fortunate that Bull Terriers are so forgiving, or there would be a great many bad-tempered ones around. 'There is no such thing as a bad Bull Terrier, only bad owners.' This is a maxim well worth remembering.

# 5

# Mature Bull Terriers

There will come a day when your dog is around two and a half years old, when you will see your Bull Terrier in a new light. No longer the rough and tumble, mischief-seeking bundle of trouble to whom you seem to have spent more time saying 'No' than anything else; instead of a long-legged, floppy eared puppy you now have an intelligent, loving and obedient companion. He will be strongly built, healthy, and of sound character and temperament. He will be a self-controlled, gentle and reliable addition to the family, his only demands to be allowed to be part of your everyday activities, a dry and draught-free bed and a regular nourishing meal.

By now you should both have come to an arrangement regarding training – he will know just how much he can get away with and you will find that a change in your tone of voice is all that is needed for him to understand when you mean business and when it is a game. Bull Terriers have telepathy. They know when you sense danger or there is an emergency and are remarkably responsive to your urgent need for them to do exactly as they are told at that moment. They are fully aware of their own physical power and inherited fighting prowess, but outwardly they have no need to show off – they remain quietly confident of their own ability. Bull Terriers are not snappy or quarrelsome. They will put up with many rude remarks from other dogs before they retaliate.

## Keeping more than one Bull Terrier in the House

You may decide to acquire a second Bull Terrier. Having once come under the spell of this special breed it is hard to resist. Many owners claim that their Bull Terrier is lonely when they are out at work all day and needs a companion. These are obviously novices to the breed. The Bull Terrier will have his home situation well in hand,

60

know just what he can and cannot get away with while the house is empty and be thankful for the regular spell of peace and quiet. He may be on his own, but he will not be lonely. He will be well aware that it is his responsibility to guard the house which has been left in his charge, and having availed himself of the most comfortable bed or chair, he will carry out his duties from a reclining position! I once spent several weeks confined to my bed and one morning the dog of that time, having seen the family off to school, quietly tiptoed upstairs (forbidden territory) and peered round the bedroom door. The amazement on his face when he discovered that this was where I had been hiding for the last couple of weeks quite outweighed any look of guilt at having been caught upstairs. Even a younger dog will take himself off to bed for a quiet sleep once he knows you have departed. He is recouping his strength for all the exciting activities that will go on once the household returns.

If life is dull and uninteresting when you return, if your Bull Terrier is expected to stay in his bed or go to his kennel with no walk or play, then of course he will have to find some entertainment while you are out and he is free to roam. Leather shoes and handbags, cushions and pillows, wires to pull and curtains to swing on, are all full of play potential. How is he to know the difference between your new pair of shoes and that old one you gave him to romp with in the garden, or between a live electric wire and the curtain cords? A Bull Terrier does not require another dog for company, he needs you! They would far rather be with you than lounging on your bed at home. He certainly does not wish to share you with any other animal, let alone another Bull Terrier. Certainly all outward signs will be of enjoyment derived from each other's company when racing around the fields together, but neither really wants to share you with the other.

Loyalty to owner and family is strong and if the reciprocal attention from you is being shared with another dog it can lead to jealousy. Most caring owners are aware of this and try not to let the situation arise. Squabbles will ensue when one dog thinks the other is about to receive a favour, such as a biscuit or having a ball thrown. Two Bull Terriers will have had to agree on the pecking order between them. Sometimes one is automatically more subservient and while this order is maintained harmony will reign. The most usual combination of this sort is mother and daughter, where it does not occur to the younger bitch to challenge her mother's authority. It is well known that adult dogs and bitches will not harm a young puppy, and it is easier therefore, to introduce a second dog into the household if it is under six months of age than to introduce an older dog. Two bitches will cohabit reasonably well but two dogs should not be expected to live together.

Eventually, there will be a fight for dominance. An older dog may have tolerated a puppy while he was young, but as in the wild, there will come a day when the puppy is no longer young and will try his strength against the adult. It usually happens around the time when the puppy reaches eight to nine months, and can be triggered off by a bitch, possibly some distance away from your premises, being in season. It could be over something that may seem trivial to you, such as an old bone or who is to be the first to have his lead put on when you have called them for an outing. Possibly the best combination for living in harmony is a dog and a bitch. Natural canine language forbids a dog to pick a fight with a bitch, it will be the female who provokes any attack.

If you feel that it is essential for you to house more than one Bull Terrier, or that it will benefit a dog, such as one in need of rescue, then be prepared and arrange your home accordingly. Insist that they have cages for their beds, housed in different rooms, as this way you can always confine one or both at any given moment. If they do disagree you may find it necessary to shut the door of one dog's cage in order to get the other one past to go outside. An excellent aid is to have a child-gate or half-gate across the hall or a doorway so that one dog can be shut into a certain area but not feel shut off from the household as he would had a door been closed. This way he can see you over the top of the gate as you pass and can hear that the other dog is not getting any more attention.

# Fighting

It is necessary to differentiate between that despicable activity known as dog fighting and two dogs having a fight. The former is growing unfortunately, and every Bull Terrier owner should be aware of the danger of having their pet stolen from their garden or car for this illegal activity. Bull Terriers have the speed, strength, power of jaw and determination to fight to the death which appeals to the villains that partake in dog fighting. Their main drawback is that they are slow to rouse and will take much punishment before they decide to retaliate. Staffordshire Bull Terriers are quicker to fight and are unfortunately therefore in greater demand. The cross-bred American Pit Bull Terrier is being used more and more however, being bred by certain groups in our society to increase fighting attributes and for activities such as badger baiting or victimisation.

We are concerned with the latter group here however – two dogs having a fight. Although we hope this will never happen, and usually in the home it is no more than a skirmish, it is sensible to be aware of what happens and the theory of what to do. The first fight I had to deal with was between two four-month-old puppies. Looking back now it seems a simple affair, but at the time the noise and ferocity of the two little mites was amazing. I had read up on what action to take should such an incident occur, but when one furious little spitfire is standing on and completely covering the other fireball it is difficult to see any part to grab hold of other than an ear at one end and a protruding tail at the other. Fortunately, while I was still dithering around the mother turned up and barged in, tossing them to either side of her with a definite cuff to the ears.

The most likely incidents in the home are those that happen when you have left a room with two Bull Terriers 'fast asleep' in their respective places (probably the two armchairs!) Some interesting toy or the suspicion that you may have left a biscuit on the empty coffee tray will be sufficient to squabble over. Maybe one has woken from a dream about fighting and wishes to continue. Often these will be no more than squabbles, the one dog being subservient to the other in their pre-arranged pecking order. Two dogs will quickly turn their skirmish into a fight however, the young adolescent flexing his muscles and the older dog determined to maintain dominance.

In the wild, dogs have a pack-leader and a pecking order so that any fighting is merely to put usurpers in their place. In one kennel, peace reigned until the matriarch (the one who had been seen to teach her pups how to fight) died. She had never been known to fight with the other kennel dogs and it had not been fully realised that it was her leadership that had kept order. Once she was no longer around, one bitch after another picked quarrels with the others, all considering themselves equally qualified to fill the old lady's role!

It is as well to be prepared for your dog to come into contact with another of meaner tendencies at some time in his life. A Bull Terrier will put up with a great deal of nonsense before retaliating, but what do you do when he decides he has to assert his authority? If an encounter takes place in a public area such as in the street or the park, there will be uninformed bystanders being of little help, and offering facile suggestions. As the owner, and therefore manager of the 'fierce' dog you will be expected to know what to do. You need to be seen to be in charge so that the handler of the other dog or any willing assistant will take instructions from you. Their natural instinct will be to pull at their dog to get him away from the 'nasty bully', even though their animal was the instigator of it all! Others look for aids – sticks to beat the dogs, buckets of water to throw over them and so on – all of which will be of no use whatsoever. The dogs merely associate any pain thus inflicted as part of the fight and you will now have two even more furious and wet dogs to deal with, as well as wet slippery ground preventing you from getting a firm footing.

The first round of a fight is full of skirmish and growling but little else. It is at this stage that many an enthusiastic helper gets bitten. Once a dog has succeeded in getting a hold of the other, the teeth are occupied and it is much safer to proceed with your efforts to put an end to the fight. Usually, they take a hold on the side of the neck or jaw of their adversary and then stand still, 'locked' together. Providing the equipment is to hand, clip a lead to the underdog's collar or if he is not wearing a collar make a noose with rope, and tie the other end to a strong source so that he is firmly tethered and cannot retaliate by sinking his teeth into you or the other dog once the grip has been loosened. If a reliable helper is available they can hold this for you, but so often it is better to use a tree or similar strong support as it will not take fright and let go of the dog, giving him a chance to get back into the fray again.

Having secured him, tighten the lead or rope and return to the dog that has the grip. Grasp him firmly by his collar and twist it but at the same time keep pushing his head towards the other dog. Keep the tension on the twisted collar and eventually he will have to let go of his adversary in order to gasp for air. When that moment comes swing him away turning your back on the tethered dog, moving away beyond the reach of his snapping jaws. Your dog must then be removed from the scene and thrust into some secure place – another room, a car or anywhere available – to prevent him returning to the action. If you have a free hand (though if the dog is an eighty pounder you may well be using it to support yourself) grab the base of his tail so that you then have control of both ends of the dog, and remove him from the area without lifting him up by his collar as this leaves the whole of his body as a target for the other dog's teeth. If the other dog does succeed in repeating the attack then you must release your dog to defend himself otherwise the attacker is likely to sink his teeth into you by mistake or obtain a hold on a vulnerable part of your dog.

As you carry him away, your dog may make high pitched gurgling noises. Do not be fooled into thinking he is being strangled and release him. This is fighting talk and he must be securely shut away from his adversary before you let him go. For safety, do not offer him any part of you to have a go at in his frustration. Rather leave him alone to cool off and return to the other dog. If the whole episode has taken place in the house or in kennels I just shut this dog in, still tethered, to think about it all. Unfortunately neither dog will forget, and they will be looking for an opportunity to finish the round! Only when they have had a chance to calm down do I then approach them to see what damage has been done.

Punctures and cuts can become infected from the germs on the other dog's teeth and would benefit from some antibiotic powder. Usually there is remarkably little damage done provided the dogs have been handled correctly. Should some 'instant expert' have tried pulling the dogs apart then serious damage will have been inflicted. Much nonsense is talked about the Bull Terrier's 'locking jaw'. The fact is that they have the strength and design to be able to hold on to an adversary once they have got a grip and yet to continue to breathe. Most other breeds need to let go eventually to draw breath. If two fighting dogs are pulled apart, the Bull Terrier will not let go – he will take the other animal's flesh with him. For this reason, if a Bull Terrier should get his teeth into a person, they should not jump and pull away – rather stay quite still until the hold is released. In this case there will only be punctures where the teeth sank in. Always push the dog into the bite rather then pull him away.

As you must realise by now prevention is better than cure and it is a wise precaution not to encourage any situation that may end up in conflict. Never leave two Bull Terriers alone in a room together. They may be perfectly happy for months on end, but a time will come when some squabble develops into a fight and perhaps even leads to the death of one of your beloved pets. Try not to walk your dogs where you know other dogs may be running free. Once a Bull Terrier has had a scrap with another dog he will be more ready to have a go with any other dog that tries to provoke him. Always keep them on a lead so that you have a restraint if aggressive dogs do approach. A flexi lead provides plenty of freedom but gives you ultimate control.

# Obedience Training

Although you have now reached a stage of compromise between yourself and your Bull Terrier as to how much he intends to admit he understands of your training programme and how much you have quietly forgotten in order to save coming into direct conflict with him, it may be rather fun to take him to obedience training school. It is a form of activity that he will enjoy as being something he does with you alone. He will look forward to these special outings where he can meet his canine friends and spend time pleasing you.

Obedience classes are more widespread in America than in Great Britain. In Great Britain, so many of the classes are held in halls that are too small and without sufficient trainers and a dog that may not prove to be a willing pupil is rather a nuisance, particularly as he is a possible disrupter of the gentler breeds who would not dream of putting a step wrong! These classes are an excellent opportunity for you to continue the socialisation of your Bull Terrier, especially if you live in a rural area where opportunities for meeting other dogs and their owners are few and far beteen. However, it must be remembered that what works for some breeds does not necessarily work for a Bull Terrier and the most benefit can be gained if your Bull Terrier knows much of the work before going to classes. They simply provide an opportunity to use it in different surroundings.

If you find that obedience work appeals to you both, you may progress to competitive work. Each dog is marked on the standard he has reached and on a points system rather than one dog against another.

## *Ringcraft*

These classes are very helpful for those owners who would like to try their hand at showing their Bull Terrier. They accustom the Bull Terrier to being among other types of dog, to confining their activities to the small space allotted to them and to being handled by different people. Again, make sure this is a fun activity to be doing with you and not a last resort to get your Bull Terrier to behave, because if it is, it will not work. A nervous or shy dog will be finished off completely if plunged headlong into this sort of situation. The only avenue left open to him seems to be aggression – the last thing you want to train him in. Everything you do together should be fun with praise as the chief reward.

# Care of the Older Dog

Hopefully your Bull Terrier will be your active companion for many years to come, but he will gradually calm down, appreciate his home comforts and while enjoying some new adventure will always be pleased to return to the security of routine. As his joints get stiff he will appreciate two short walks rather than one long one; a trip in the car to favourite haunts rather than having to walk the entire distance and then being too tired to enjoy the destination; a rug on the patio for lying in the sun instead of direct on to the concrete with all its draughty currents of cold air; an extra padding of blanket for his bedding to ease sore joints and a bed with sides high enough to ensure that no draughts can get at him.

If healthy, an older dog will still have a very good appetite, but it is a wise precaution to make sure that he does not get overweight, putting unnecessary stress on limbs and organs. With less activity his diet should be adjusted accordingly. He still needs the extra vitamins and additives to keep him healthy but he will not require such a high protein diet. Ears require regular checks, eyes are prone to problems as old age sets in, and toe-nails are likely to need filing quite frequently now that the road work is not really sufficient to keep them short.

## *Ears*

These should be kept clean and any build-up of wax washed out with ear-drops. Normally the wax dries out and is shed from the ear during the course of normal activities, but if there is considerable shaking of the ears, or scratching, then it is a sign that the dog needs help in keeping the situation under control. Never poke around in the ears, but use a proprietary medicinal cleanser sold for the purpose. Violent shaking of the head can lead to a knock on the ear-flaps resulting in a ruptured blood vessel. This haematoma or blood-blister will need to be lanced and drained by a veterinary surgeon and stitched or left to disperse naturally. With great care the repair job can be such a success that the ear trumpet remains upright with no more than a thickening of scar tissue. If left to disperse naturally the ear becomes distorted (known as a 'cauliflower ear'). No other harm is caused and for this reason it is best to leave the blood-blister to disperse naturally in the elderly dog rather than expect the dog to undergo unnecessary surgical treatment.

## Eyes

If your Bull Terrier's eyesight is gradually failing it is up to you to compensate for this by remembering to talk to him when you approach, not to leave obstacles in unusual places and to make large arm movements that he might see or so that he can feel the air current. If your normally placid Bull Terrier starts giving slight grumbles or mutterings it is worthwhile checking his eyesight. It is often a sign that he is feeling insecure as to what is going on around him, and he is giving a warning that he is there, just in case an adversary is approaching. If there are other dogs on the premises he will need assurance when entering another room or outdoors that it is all clear for him – he may even want you to accompany him. He will be quite content provided the surroundings remain familiar as he knows where the doorways and steps are to be found. When walking outside however, he must be kept on a lead, even though he may never stir from your heel. He needs the added confidence that you are there on the end of the lead guiding and caring for him. He will need talking to as you go along, telling when you reach the curb or when another dog is approaching. Always remember to speak to him before touching him. With thought on your part a blind Bull Terrier can lead a happy and normal life and you will be surprised how many onlookers are not aware of his failing eyesight.

## Teeth

Teeth need to be kept clean as they gather a hard build-up of tartar with age. If it gets really bad the veterinary surgeon will show you how to scrape them clean keeping the breath fresh. If the teeth are neglected they could become badly decayed and an abcess may form, causing swelling and general blood poisoning. A regular supply of hard biscuits and an occasional marrow bone (removed before it can be cracked or chipped and cause trouble if bits are swallowed), will help to keep the teeth healthy and give him something to occupy part of his day.

## Skin Problems

These can be caused by mites, fleas, an allergy or inheritance. The first two can be traced and dealt with and avoiding action taken in the case of allergies, but inherited skin problems are more difficult. It is widely thought that they are more prevalent in white Bull Terriers, but this may be the result of being able to see a skin lesion more easily on a white dog. The coloured Bull Terrier is quite as capable of carrying the problem for future generations. Occasional treatment by your veterinary surgeon with cortisone will keep the worst conditions in abeyance while an alternative treatment is found for your Bull Terrier. Various animal veterinary establishments are carrying out research in this area. In the meantime, the condition has to be dealt with on a day to day basis, and the problem contained if possible. The scabs should be bathed in warm water and the area dried. Then apply some antibiotic powder or a drying agent such as surgical spirit. The dog must be thoroughly inspected every day and each new spot treated at the first sign. This way the problem can be kept under control.

## Heart Problems

Heart problems can have been present since birth, inherited from the parents. These may have been discovered at a routine check at the veterinary surgeon's. Such a puppy is often the smallest in the litter and does not grow at the same rate as his brothers and sisters. In the older dog often the only indication is a heart murmur diagnosed by the vet. As the heart gets worse, there may be visible signs of heart failure – a cough (caused by congestion of the lungs), which is more apparent after excitement or on first getting up after a rest, less ability to take part in active exercise and in some cases swollen limbs (as the circulation slows). Another heart disease affects the muscle and nerves surrounding the heart and can result in fainting. If the dog is overweight, a reducing diet is essential and a course of drugs can improve the heart's performance and reduce fluid retention. Treatment usually has to be continued for the rest of the dog's life, but the quality of life will be greatly improved.

## *Kidney Failure*

Kidney failure is not a breed-specific disease or even confined to dogs, and there are various causes. It is not solely a hereditary disease though this is the cause most talked about as it is most often diagnosed in dogs under two years old. It is in the area of inheritance that research may be of benefit to future generations. However, a dog can acquire infections and poisons at any age which lodge in the kidneys causing failure. Outward signs of this are vomiting, high temperature and tiredness.

It is a disease which can go undetected for some time in the older dog. If the dog is generally under the weather, losing weight and energy he may be in the early stages of kidney failure. Another sign is if he is drinking large quantities of water. By taking a sample of the dog's urine for testing the veterinary surgeon will be able to determine whether or not a blood test should be made. Later, blood will be seen being passed in the urine, but usually by this stage it is obvious that there is something wrong.

Throughout a dog's life care should be taken to keep toxic substances such as household cleaners and garden sprays – weed killers and insecticides – away from animal exercise areas. Danger can lurk not only on your own premises, but outside where grass verges and park paths have been sprayed with chemicals, or farmers have been spraying to reduce weeds. Some sprays are active for up to three weeks after their application. Not only is there a risk of contamination from airborne sprays but also from contact when a dog is sniffing around sprayed plants or rolling in long sprayed grass. If in any doubt, on the return from a likely infected area, wash down your Bull Terrier's paws and undercarriage before he goes to rest. Some of the sprays are irritants and he will want to spend the time licking himself, thus ingesting the poisons. A build-up of these in the kidneys can damage these organs.

Give a careful, low-protein diet, plenty of rest at a reasonably constant temperature together with gentle exercise and your Bull Terrier should be able to remain in a fairly stable condition.

Bull Terriers are very tough and can become quite ill before anyone notices anything is the matter. A thermometer is a very good indicator of the health of your dog. Any infection can be detected in this way. It may be that after a lot of activity he is just preferring a day in bed but as he ages so his resistance to infection will lower.

## *Diet*

Dogs will eat anything, whether it is a dead seagull on the beach or lettuce leaves – I have just witnessed my eleven-year-old bitch devour these for the first time in her life! However, the object of feeding your dog is to provide a diet which will retain good health, without promoting obesity. If, from some other cause such as arthritis, he no longer takes very much exercise, he may lose his appetite and become too thin. It may then be necessary to persuade him to eat by providing his favourite foods but in small amounts. Eggs, cooked liver and milk will all help tempt him to eat, and a sprinkling of grated cheese over his dinner is also often an excellent inducement. Two or three small meals a day are often more acceptable than one large meal. He needs protein but not in the same quantity as when he was a growing, active youngster, so replace red meat with white meat. Food should be something to look forward to now that his activities no longer include chasing round the garden, answering the door or running up and down stairs minding everybody's business.

At any age, but particularly when they are older, I give all the dogs a turn at roaming around the herb beds where they can help themselves to anything they fancy. One dark, damp night one of the bitches had been sick in her run, so while cleaning up I let her have a turn in the garden. She was very busy in one particular corner, and in daylight we discovered that the entire mint bed had been decapitated. There was no sign of debris so she must have eaten the lot! However she appeared fit and well so she evidently knew what it was she needed!

# 6

# Showing

## The Purpose of Dog Shows

For many dog lovers shows provide a fascinating hobby. Many miles are travelled, new parts of the country visited and friendships made with people of similar interest. The object of exhibiting is to improve the breed, giving breeders a means of comparing their stock with that of other breeders and thus furthering an interest in producing sound dogs. Dog shows are sometimes compared to beauty shows, but they are more than that, for the exhibit not only has to look his best he must also be a sound specimen of his breed in keeping with the Breed Standard.

It was in the 1860s that Bull Terriers first appeared in any show-ring. Mr James Hinks showed and won with a bitch 'Puss' that had fought and won in the fighting-ring that morning! Over the years it became the handsome, gladiatorial aspects of the Bull Terrier that held the breeders' attention and the popularity of dog shows developed.

There is little financial reward to be gained through showing other than the implied advertisement for stock or for the stud dog (puppies may grow up to look like the specimen in the ring). Of course it is a great pleasure to be presented with a card or even a trophy, but it is not mere 'pot hunting' that gives the incentive to continue in the show-ring, for many do not achieve such high honours. Rather it is the reflection on the breeding of your exhibit, the care and training you have lavished on it, and your handling skill in the ring that is being rewarded.

# Types of Show

Dog shows are held by various canine clubs and societies under the jurisdiction of the Kennel Club of Great Britain. There are four categories of dog show that come under Kennel Club rules – Exemption Shows, Limit and Sanction Shows, Open Shows and Championship Shows.

## *Exemption Shows*

As the title suggests, these are exempt from Kennel Club regulations. They still have to have a licence however, and may include in their programme up to four of the ten listed Kennel Club classes for pedigree dogs. These are:

1 Any Variety Sporting Dogs
2 Any Variety Hounds
3 Any Variety Gundogs
4 Any Variety Terriers
5 Any Variety Non-Sporting Dogs
6 Any Variety Utility
7 Any Variety Working
8 Any Variety Toys
9 Any Variety Puppy (6–12 months)
10 Any Variety Open

A fifth class may be held for pedigree dogs which are shown by exhibitors under eighteen years old. Pedigree dogs entering any of these classes need not necessarily be registered with the Kennel Club. Under certain conditions, Obedience classes may also be scheduled, though Bull Terriers are not noted as stars in this field!

Besides the above classes an unlimited number of classes are available for both pedigree and non-pedigree dogs who may or may not be registered with the Kennel Club. These may include Dog and Child Egg and Spoon Races, The Dog with the Waggiest Tail, or The Dog Most Like its Owner. These classes enable dogs who are not registered to enter, and provide an opportunity for family pets and rescued dogs who no longer have evidence of registration, to take part in events. Shows are usually held during the summer and in aid of a charity.

Although registered canine societies may not hold Exemption

73

Shows, these shows with four breed classes for Bull Terriers are held by organisations such as the Bull Terrier Club Welfare Scheme and various of the regional Bull Terrier clubs, to raise funds for the care and rescue of Bull Terriers in need of help. They raise considerable sums of money as well as providing a fun day for Bull Terriers and their canine friends who would not normally enter the showring, or whose showing days are long gone. Veteran classes are always well attended; so too is the Fancy Dress for Handler and Dog, some appearing as Little Red Riding Hood and the Wolf, Cowboys and Indians, or Beefeaters!

## Limit and Sanction Shows

These shows are limited to members of the club or society or else confined to exhibitors who reside within a specified area. Sanction Shows, with up to twenty-five classes, rarely specify Bull Terriers as one of their breed classes. Limit Shows have between twenty and forty classes and occasionally include Bull Terrier classes. Dogs who have gained a Kennel Club of Great Britain Challenge Certificate are not permitted to enter these shows. Some of the regional Bull Terrier clubs hold Limit Shows for their members, offering an opportunity for exhibits or exhibitors new to the ring to try their paces without competition from highly qualified, experienced dogs.

## Open Shows

There are often classes for Bull Terriers scheduled at Open Shows, where up to three hundred classes cater for different breeds. The Open Shows run by the various regional Bull Terrier clubs throughout Great Britain are well attended and the competition is strong. Bull Terrier owners will travel long distances to visit club shows out of their own region. If no class is available for Bull Terriers, they can be exhibited in the Any Variety classes, such as Any Variety Puppy or Any Variety Terriers. These are often tough classes with seventy or more entries, which can be tiring for young stock.

## Championship Shows

There are twenty-six General Championship Shows including Cruft's at which Kennel Club of Great Britain Challenge Certificates are available for certain breeds. These shows are subdivided into six groups – Working, Utility, Gundog, Terrier, Hound and Toy dogs. The Bull Terrier belongs to the Terrier group. The six groups will be scheduled over three or four days, the groups rotating so that Terriers do not appear on the same day each year. Then there are Group Shows which schedule only one of the groups, such as the National Terrier Club Championship Show.

Championship Shows are held by the Bull Terrier Club anually. The Yorkshire Bull Terrier Club also has permission to hold Championship Shows every year, and various regional clubs hold them on alternate years. General and Group Shows are benched shows, but breed clubs often have Kennel Club permission to be 'unbenched'.

Over the three or four days at a General Championship Show there will be several thousand dogs with high hopes of being chosen, but the Bull Terrier classes are often quite small. There can be as few as five or six Bull Terriers in any one class. Breed Club Championship Shows, on the other hand, often have large classes. There have been known to be thirty-two in Puppy Bitch class – after all where better to display stock you consider worthy of competing for Championship status than amongst and in view of breed fanciers who will appreciate the finer points of your Bull Terrier? At the General Championship Shows, there are often Any Variety Terrier or Puppy or Veteran classes. These are all well attended and do give your stock a second opportunity in the show-ring. There may also be Specials, Stake classes, or a round of the Pup of the Year competition. All are interesting to watch and to enter, but they are held after the breed classes and young dogs may become bored or tired after the early start to the day and owners may prefer to start their long journey home as soon as possible rather then stay to watch the rest of the show.

The winner (known as Best of Breed) in each breed goes forward to represent his breed in the appropriate group, for example the Bull Terrier and the Miniature Bull Terrier take part in the Terrier group. The winner of that group then competes with those from the five other groups for the Best in Show. This may mean staying overnight or coming back on the last day of the show.

# Which Show for your Bull Terrier?

General Championship Shows are held throughout Great Britain and are spread through the year commencing with the Kennel Club's own show, Cruft's, in London in mid-February and concluding with the Ladies' Kennel Association Show in Birmingham in mid-December. Advertisements for all types of show can be found in the canine press, giving the addresses from which to obtain schedules and entry forms. The Kennel Club publishes a Show Guide/Diary annually which lists the shows chronologically and gives the addresses of the Secretaries. It is essential to apply for a schedule in plenty of time as entries close a month to six weeks before the date of the show.

The Honorary Secretaries of the regional Bull Terrier clubs will provide you with details of their show dates and venues and send you a schedule upon request. Agricultural shows with a dog section and local dog shows may not necessarily advertise nationally but can be found in the local press.

The type of show that you will most enjoy depends on what you hope to gain by entering the show circuit. Some people enjoy the whole scene so much that so long as they are taking an active part, whether showing or as a spectator, they do not mind whether their choice of exhibit is successful or not. Some like to fit in as many shows as possible, making vast journeys from one end of the country to another. Being away from home every weekend is part of the fun – part of their holidays. At the other end of the scale are the exhibitors whose livelihood depends on the selling of their stock, which is advertised by being seen in the show-ring, preferably winning classes, Challenge Certificates and Best in Show.

We can dismiss this latter group for now by pointing out that they are there for the best of their stock to be seen and to be compared with that of other breeders. They hope to be among the honours for the day. Visitors may wish to purchase future stock or use the services of the stud dog that produces such exhibits. They wish to further the name of their kennel.

The rest of us need to decide why we wish to enter the show world. We all know that our own Bull Terrier is the best there could possibly be for us and for our requirements, but we all enjoy an opportunity to show the rest of the world how well he behaves, how fit we have kept him through good food and the correct amount of exercise and how well turned out he is. We wonder how he compares with other Bull Terriers, particularly if there are not many living in the neighbourhood. The occasional visit to the breeder is comforting for assurance that he is developing as he should, but it is time he went out into the world and met his peers.

A trip to the nearest Exemption Show will give you an idea of his first reactions to other dogs all more or less behaving in a ring and allowing a judge to look at them. Possibly a few more lessons at home and more small shows would be advisable before trying a breed class. Having dipped a toe in the water it is up to you to decide whether you want to paddle or swim. The breeder will often advise you – after all it is their stock that you are advertising. Maybe your dog is still too immature – another four or five months will make a great difference to his competitive status. You may decide that the show-ring is not for your Bull Terrier, in which case try some other activity such as jogging, rambling or obedience work. However, it is still worthwhile belonging to a breed club and going along to shows as a spectator as the sight of all those Bull Terriers in one place makes you appreciate your own all the more, and where better to discuss with fellow owners the various problems that have worried you.

Once you start being placed among 'the Cards' (as the first four winning places are known), you invariably get bitten by the show bug and it is then that you need to decide on your campaign. Is showing just going to be a happy day out meeting new, like-minded people and returning with the occasional trophy, or is it clear, after only a few shows, that you have a possible Challenge Certificate winner sitting in your kitchen? If this is the case, you will need to decide what you require from the whole exercise and just how much you wish to be committed. Weigh up the various aspects and plan your campaign. You will find that whatever your conclusions there will be shows suitable for you. Decide on your ultimate goal. Is it to make your Bull Terrier into a Champion or is having a good day out with all the family the more important? You must consider how often your life-style and other commitments leave you free to attend shows, how often you want to be involved in a show. Maybe you would rather breed a litter of puppies so that you would have another Bull Terrier to show in a year's time, in which case you will need to be at home rather than chasing around the show circuit.

You should also take account of financial considerations. These are divided into two sections – that paid at the time of entering the show and that which is spent on the day of the show. As these are often six weeks apart it is easy to forget the true cost of any excursion.

# Entry costs

Fees for entering a class vary from show to show, but certainly the cost is far greater to enter a class offering Challenge Certificates at a General Championship Show than to enter a similar class at a Breed Club Championship Show. Open and Limited Shows run by regional clubs and canine societies cost considerably less and for members of the organising club there is a further reduction per class.

**Admission Fee** An entry pass is provided for the dog handler – one pass for one or two dogs and two passes for three or more dogs, as you are surely going to require a second pair of hands. Any accompanying assistant such as your driver, husband, wife, partner or children have to be paid for. Extra admission tickets can sometimes be purchased in advance with the entries, at a slightly lower fee than at the gate on the day of the show.

**Car-Park** This is usually an extra payment and carries no guarantee of a place or of being adjacent to the show site. However, the general spectators' car-park tends to be even further away and a car-park pass is a necessity.

**Caravans** Some of the General Championship Shows have caravan areas and it is possible to pay for permission to park there for however many nights you require.

**Catalogue** These can sometimes be paid for in advance with your entry. The catalogue is to a dog show what a programme is to a theatrical production. It lists the classes and exhibits for your breed with their ring numbers and gives the names of the exhibitors and breeding details of the exhibits. A quick glance will reassure you that you are definitely entered in the classes of your choice and you will be able to sum up the opposition in those classes.

These catalogues are costly to print and those for some General Championship Shows, stretching over four days, are split into sections – one for each day – to lessen the necessary charge per section. Some shows print six sections – one for each of the groups into which the dogs are categorised. At other shows exhibitors in different breeds club together to buy one catalogue, dividing the relevant sections between them. At breed club shows and canine society shows the catalogue has usually been produced locally, and therefore carries a lower price.

Most of the four aforementioned can be paid for at the time of entry. The Show Secretary will send you a catalogue voucher that may be exchanged for a catalogue on entering the show, a car-park sticker for display on your windscreen which assists the attendants in directing you to the correct car-park, and extra admission tickets, all of which help you to reach your destination with the least amount of hold-ups. These advance payments also provide a nucleus of income for the show management who have colossal printing and labour expenses to cover before the big day arrives. Fortunately for exhibitors, most of these expenses have been met well in advance so that the actual expenses of the day never seem quite as much as they actually are.

# Day of Show Expenses

**Travel**  As shows can involve two or three hundred mile return journeys, petrol costs and toll-bridge/road charges will all mount up, and even if you share a car with exhibitors in another breed, you still have to get to the pick-up point.

Coach tour operators occasionally organise coach parties to the bigger venues and of course to Cruft's. Sometimes, canine societies will hire a coach for the use of their members and friends. This may drive a very circuitous route in order to cover as many pick-up points as possible, but at least it is a comfortable means of transport and does not leave you worn out from a long and difficult drive before you even start on the business of showing your dog. It is becoming a very popular way of getting to Cruft's where reaching the car-parks is so difficult. I suspect however, that much of the success of coach travel depends on what your Bull Terrier thinks of it. If he can agree that it is a good day out and he is not going to be travel-sick, then you can enjoy the trip too.

**Sustenance**   Allowance needs to be made not only for sustenance at the show, but for meals *en route* and maybe even overnight. When going to the outdoor, summer General Championship Shows, we tow the caravan, park it in the caravan park, stay for the three or four days of the show, visiting the sights of the neighbourhood as well as seeing the different groups each day, and enjoying a thoroughly good break.

**Kennel Staff**   If you have left a large number of dogs at home, then someone will have to look after them, whether you are away for a few hours or several days. This is where those with adult relations living at home or competent live-in staff score. The rest of us have to pay kennel staff for the extra hours worked and this should be counted in with show expenses.

**Purchases**   General Shows are an opportunity to stock up with supplies of dog food, dishes, collars and so forth. Although these items are part of kennel management it is still an outlay made at shows. Then there may well be memorabilia or gifts that you wish to purchase for people at home. You may wish to buy further supplies of breed headed stationery, visit the Pet Insurance stand to pay your premium, the Kennel Club stand for their various forms and publications, or one of the publishing stands to get more pedigree forms for your forthcoming litter.

It is therefore increasingly clear that financial aspects cannot be ignored when planning your show campaign, otherwise what should be an enjoyable if time-consuming hobby, could become a burden.

You may decide that this grand-scale excursion around the show circuit is not for you, in which case the one-day breed club shows may be the answer. The Open Shows run by these clubs are inexpensive to enter and the catalogue price will have been kept as low as possible. You will be expected to purchase their delicious home-made refreshments, as it is the arduous efforts of their committee in this direction that subsidises the running costs of the show! A club stand usually has the necessary show paraphernalia such as nylon show leads and ring number clips as well as some Bull Terrier models and club badges, for sale. Each club usually runs a raffle for club funds or in support of charity or the Bull Terrier Welfare Scheme, and occasionally members give items of special value to Bull Terrier fanciers which are auctioned from the ring during the lunch- or tea-break. You may have travelled from one side of Britain to the other, or even from one state to another in North America, but the expense of the actual show will not be so great as at the larger All Breed Shows.

Similarly, considerable fun and experience both for handler and young stock can be found by attending the local canine society Open Show. There may not be a class for Bull Terriers but you can enter in Any Variety Terrier, Any Variety Puppy and so forth.

Occasionally, dogs seem to be happier, more extrovert and there-fore better showmen at some shows rather than others. Dogs may suffer from long distance travel, for example. Some dogs are hap-pier out of doors than indoors, and it is very difficult to simulate an indoor show-hall for acclimatising the dogs during training. Such aspects as lighting, the closeness of the audience and the other dogs in the ring or slipping on polished floors can make dogs feel very insecure. The acoustics – the barking and noise of all the chatter – can also be very alarming. At the General Championship Shows the buildings are so large that the echo is similar to that heard at a swimming-pool. If your dog is affected by any of this, then the venue should be a deciding factor when considering which show to visit, at least until your dog is so used to the whole activity that the stress caused by one type of venue is no longer foremost in his mind. Most of us end up by attending a mixture of all three types of show (not necessarily with the same dog) depending on what we require from our hobby of dog showing.

# 7

# Entering a Show – The Preliminaries

Any pure-bred dog registered at the Kennel Club of Great Britain can enter a show provided he is over six months old and a suitable class for which he qualifies is being offered. Having obtained your schedule from the Honorary Show Manager or the Honorary Secretary of the organising body, you will find the most important information set out on the front cover – the date of the show, the venue and the closing date for entry. I usually mark these with a highlighter pen so that they stand out from the rest of the information. Inside will be the details of the Kennel Club Rules and Regulations, classification and definitions of the classes being offered, information regarding particular competitions such as Best Puppy in Show and Best in Show and of any special invitation competitions that may be taking place at the show.

An entry form is provided with the schedule. One or two of the General Championship Shows have taken a double-page spread in the canine press printing the entire schedule and an entry form. This saves the enormous expense of printing and posting the schedules. Others allow any dog show entry form (suitably adapted), to be used to enter their show. All require the full registered name of the dog, the breed, sex, date of birth and name of breeder (if the breeder and the owner are the same person this column is filled in as 'owner'). The next two columns are for the name of the exhibit's sire and dam and lastly, there is a column for the numbers of the classes to be entered as stated in the schedule. If the Kennel Club registration of the name of the dog has not been returned to you at the time of making your entry (possibly it is in the process of having an affix added) then the initials 'N.A.F.' are added after the entry in the Registered Name column. This stands for 'name applied for' and should the same predicament arise over the transfer to your ownership 'T.A.F.' can be inserted ('transfer applied for'). Now that the kennel Club has completed the change-over to computerisation, registrations do not take long to be completed and there is less need to add these initials. Finally, there is a declaration to be signed and dated by the owner agreeing to abide by the Kennel Club Rules and Regulations under which the show is being run. This includes agreeing not to exhibit any animal that has been in contact with infectious diseases during the six weeks prior to the date of the show, and that any dogs you propose to exhibit will have been prepared for the show-ring as per the requirements of the Kennel Club Regulations for the Preparation of Dogs for Exhibition. You may be expected to fill in your address three times – one for reference and the others to act as address labels for sending your entry pass and next year's schedule. (It will be sent out automatically to all the previous year's exhibitors.)

It is essential to write clearly or to type the details on the form as an incorrect name could mean disqualification from that show and any awards gained would be taken back. If on receiving your catalogue, you find an error, a mis-copied name or date of birth, a visit to the Show Secretary's office before the class commences can quickly put things right. Although you will be anxious to get the facts put right, try to avoid attacking the Secretary for a mistake on the part of the office or the printers – it may have been your own fault. I once entered my dog in the bitch class and his litter sister in the corresponding dog class! If you enter your dog incorrectly in a class which has an age qualification, such as a Puppy or Junior class then he may not be transferred to his correct class – rather only to the Open class. The Minor Puppy class is an exception, as an age error here can be transfered to the Puppy class. Clearly, it pays to fill in the entry forms at a time when interruptions will be few and the distractions of the telephone and television can be avoided.

The closing date for entries must be adhered to. If they are late the Secretary will return them. Most societies accept the postal date as proof of posting within the allotted time, which relieves the worry of postal delays, though it is much better to form the habit of sending entries off leaving plenty of time. If you are in the midst of a run of shows it is difficult to send in any earlier than seven days because of the calculation of wins. It might be worth taking your entry to the Post Office and obtaining a free Certificate of Posting. This will at least be some form of proof that the entry left you. A stamped, self-addressed postcard can be enclosed so that you re-ceive confirmation of receipt of entries if you are really concerned.

Deciding which class to enter is fairly straightforward to begin with but as your exhibit collects wins it becomes rather like a game of chess. The classes are listed in the schedule with their class number and there is a printed list of Definition of Classes.

# Definition of Classes

**Minor Puppy**  For dogs of six and not exceeding nine calendar months of age on the first day of the show.

All entries must be at least six months old. Many feel that we are inclined to show our Bull Terriers too soon, so that they have finished their show career before reaching maturity. Very few shows hold Minor Puppy classes for Bull Terriers, but where they do, it usually attracts a good proportion of youngsters trying out their paces without the competition of the more advanced animals of nine to twelve months old.

**Puppy**  For dogs of six and not over twelve months old on the first day of the show.

This is a good class in that the dog is still learning and misbehaviour through lack of practice and experience is easily tolerated, whereas exhibits in an older class should know what is expected of them in the ring and variations are not so likely to be smiled upon. After spending many months with my first show puppy travelling to every little Exemption Show and far-flung agricultural Open Shows, I eventually risked a Puppy class at a Bull Terrier Club Show, only to be amazed at their misbehaviour.

**Juniors**  For dogs of six and not over eighteen months old on the first day of the show.

This can be a quality and highly competitive class and is not really one for a pup just learning the craft. Some entries could have won several Challenge or Reserve Challenge Certificates. It is not unknown, however, for a pup of high calibre to come through from the Puppy class and snatch the trophy!

**Yearling**  For dogs of six months and not over two years old on the first day of the show.

It is very unlikely that one of these classes will be offered for Bull Terriers.

**Maiden**   For dogs who have not won a Challenge Certificate or a first prize at an Open or Championship Show (Puppy and Minor Puppy dogs are often excepted here).

**Novice**   For dogs who have not won a Challenge Certificate or three or more first prizes at Open and Championship Shows.

Both the Maiden and the Novice classes are very popular with those dogs now too old to compete in Puppy and Junior classes and those who do not aspire to great heights in the show-ring, but who enjoy a day at a show with an occasional win. The competitive aspect will become more intense if a win in such a class means the dog will qualify for entry to Cruft's Dog Show (a qualification that varies from year to year). Note that the qualification includes wins at both Open and Championship Shows.

**Graduate**   For dogs who have not won a Challenge Certificate or four or more first prizes at Championship Shows in Graduate, Post Graduate, Limit and Open classes.

**Post Graduate**   For dogs who have not won a Challenge Certificate or five or more first prizes at Championship Shows in Post Graduate, Limit and Open classes.

**Limit**   For dogs who have not won three Challenge Certificates under three different judges or seven or more first prizes in all at Championship Shows in Limit and Open classes, confined to the breed.

**Open**   For all dogs who are eligible for entry to the show and of the breed for which the class is intended.

This class is really only for the cream of the breed, most competitors being too qualified for the other classes. At a Championship Show this is where the 'big boys' appear – all the Bull Terrier dogs and bitches that are in contention for a Challenge Certificate. However, there are occasions when this class is poorly supported and a novice may collect a second or third placing which is qualification for entry into the stud-book, which in turn is sometimes one of the listed qualifications for entry to Cruft's Dog Show.

**Veteran**   For dogs of seven years or older on the first day of the show.

This varies from show to show. At Championship Shows the qualifying age is seven years, but at some Open Shows it is five years. It is an enjoyable class with the elderly Bull Terriers appreciating a trip back into the show-ring, and it provides an opportunity for the spectators to see mature Bull Terriers.

**Brace** For two exhibits (of one sex or mixed) of one breed, belonging to the same exhibitor, each exhibit having been entered in some class other than Brace or Team.

**Special Beginners** For dogs and bitches shown by an exhibitor whose dogs have never won a Challenge Certificate in the breed.
    This class is one for which the exhibitor has to qualify, not the Bull Terrier.

**Variety classes** A Variety class is one in which more than one breed and varieties of a breed can compete. A dog is not eligible for entry unless entered and exhibited in a breed class.

To decide which classes you are eligible for, it is helpful to keep a careful record of which shows you have entered, the classes and any wins, second or third placings. At first it seems unnecessary – after all, you remember the thrill of receiving that first silver cup and you do not feel you need to record it anywhere – but there will come a day when you will want to count up your points towards the Junior Warrant, or you are not sure whether you have won six or seven first prizes. Then you will wish that you had been more methodical with your record-keeping. Particular note should be made of whether the Show was a Limit, Open or Championship.
    In estimating the number of prizes won, all wins up to seven days before the closing date for entries should be counted. This becomes more complicated where Variety classes are concerned. To enter these, wins in both Breed and Variety classes must be counted. However, wins in Variety classes do not count for entry in Breed classes.
    Having completed your form, ordered any extra passes, car-park pass, catalogue ticket and whatever else may be on offer, total it up and write out your cheque. Before sealing the envelope make a note of the details on the front cover of the schedule. On return from the Post Office, staple the Certificate of Posting to your schedule and then all will be in one place. In six weeks time you can check which dogs are entered for which classes.

Ten to fourteen days before the date of the show you will receive your Entrance Pass and various sheets of information such as the order in which the breeds are to appear in the ring, benching arrangements, as well as any other tickets you may have ordered. If you do not receive this and it is getting near to the show date, check your bank statement to see if the cheque has been cleared. The Show Secretary is reaching the busiest time so if you contact him/her, have all your facts ready – breed, how many dogs entered, total amount of money sent, details of what that money covered and whether the cheque has been presented to your bank yet. When the tickets do arrive, put them with the show bag. They will not be much good to you left behind on the kitchen table. One couple arrived at a show, after an exciting night during which their first grandchild was born, only to realise that they had not brought their passes. They visited the Secretary's tent and the trouble was overcome. In the ring that day their Bull Terrier went on to win his third Challenge Certificate, making him up to Champion – what a day!

## Preparation for a Show

If your Bull Terrier is to do you and the breed justice when he enters the ring, much preparatory work must be carried out. You should start when your dog is around three months old. He will need to have plenty of exercise and a careful diet to ensure that he is in top condition, outshining all those around him with the vigour and showmanship that comes with a healthy condition. Time and effort will have been necessary to train him to the standards of the show-ring.

### *Ringcraft*

You can start training your puppy as soon as he moves into his new home with you. Noises of every kind – electric vacuum cleaners, radio, television and traffic – should be part of his general training, each being introduced quietly at first so that he does not become a nervous wreck. To prepare him for the crowds and noises of the showground he should be gently introduced to people, walking amongst ever increasing numbers. Once used to meeting my friends and neighbours when out for a walk on the lead, I take my puppy for a walk each day at the time when the local school is emptying out.

At first we observe them from afar, then we walk out at a time when most of the children have gone so that there are only a few tired stragglers to pass and eventually we can happily walk in the same direction as or against the main flow. It is often difficult to reproduce the sounds heard at an indoor dog show. The echo is akin to that heard at an indoor swimming-pool, with innumerable dogs barking sharps and flats. To walk past the school playground when the juniors are playing is just about the noisiest place in town! I have even stood in a bus queue when not really intending to make a journey, and in an ice-cream queue. Familiarity with such surroundings will make life a lot easier when it comes to taking your dog through the gates to a show where tickets are being checked and everyone is anxious to get to their destination as soon as possible with their dogs and all their baggage.

Training is necessary to ensure that your Bull Terrier will exhibit all his potential qualities to the best advantage when shown. You may know that you have the finest dog, but he must be shown properly or he will be at a grave disadvantage. A dog who will not allow the judge to handle him, who pulls away or behaves stupidly when being shown will not do himself justice. Led by the handler, the dog should show himself off giving the judge every chance to appreciate all his good qualities.

Ten minutes instruction every day is of far more value to the dog than an hour one day and then no more for long intervals. The dog should have a good play or romp before you start a training session as this should take some of the bounce out of him and make him more amenable and attentive. Use titbits as rewards if he is doing well as this not only encourages him but teaches him to watch your hands. Do most of your training with your hand. Shouting or using a loud or excitable voice only excites and unnerves a dog. A firm sharp tone of voice is much more effective than any hint of unkindness which could destroy the dog's trust in you. You must always be very patient – never lose your temper. If you begin to feel irritable because you think your Bull Terrier is being stupid, stop the training for a few minutes and then start again.

To start with, play with the puppy, then put a lead on him and walk slowly across the space where you are teaching him, making him keep to your left heel. As you do this say the word 'heel' very clearly over and over again. A great deal of patience is needed with a Bull Terrier to make him understand what is required of him. He will appear dull-witted, obstinate and quite determined to misunderstand the essence of the activity! Keep him on your left, never allowing him to cross to your right side. This is easier in a space such as your garden, as outside he will be inclined to swerve from one interesting sniff to another – from tree to lampost and back again! Gradually you will find that you can loosen the lead until he is keeping to your left heel without any control. Once he seems to have mastered this exercise, try taking him out on to the pavement for a walk. When you see another dog coming, repeat the word 'heel' in the same quiet tone so he knows that he must pay attention only to you. If he tries to pull ahead, gently pull him back saying the word 'heel' in a firm clear voice. If it is difficult to cure him of pulling, take a folded newspaper with you and when he tries to forge ahead give him a tap on the nose with the paper.

It is best to keep him on the lead for all his early lessons as he will be on a lead in the show-ring and he should be thoroughly accustomed to its use. Take him to an area where you can walk him in a circle of a size similar to that of a show-ring, getting him used to moving at an easy pace and making sure that he stays on the side nearest to the judge who will be in the centre of the ring. Bull Terrier judges in Great Britain do not expect to move the exhibits around the ring in a circle at the beginning of each class as they recognise that Bull Terriers do not do themselves justice during this particular exercise. However, all-rounder judges are used to moving other breeds in this way, as are judges in other countries, so it is as well that your dog knows how to do it, in case you should wish to show under one of these judges.

Next take the dog to the end of a pathway and make him walk, slowly at first, in a straight line down it. Practise this repeatedly, so acclimatising the dog to moving easily in a straight line across a ring. Eventually he will automatically turn at the end of the path and without losing his stride or propulsion will return along the same route. Finally, teach him to walk the three sides of a triangle, turning at the corner angles so that the stride is not broken and so that he remains on the side nearest the judge the whole time. The judge will be looking for drive and impulsion so the dog needs to be kept on the move and not be pulling and swerving all over a ring which makes it very difficult for any judge to see how he really moves. Watch the tail carriage to see that it is correct – horizontally out behind. Run your hand down his back and along the tail to encourage him to carry it correctly. Talk to him and when he does an exercise well praise him. Most dogs love to be praised.

When you have taught your dog to walk in a circle and in a straight line bring your heeling lesson into practice. Say 'heel', then stop and make the dog stop instantly remaining standing where he is. Carry in your hand some small titbit and when he does well, reward him. Do most of your training with your hands so that the dog knows what you want him to do by watching them.

## Preparing your Dog for a Show

Three or four days before a show, your Bull Terrier should be bathed. He should have had regular baths since puppyhood to ensure that he does not find this procedure alarming. All of my dogs know that there is some outing afoot if baths are on the timetable. Coloured Bull Terriers can often get away with fewer baths, provided they have a healthy and shining coat which can be buffed up with a velvet or chamois-leather cloth. Then only the white parts need be sponged clean and they are ready. White Bull Terriers (particularly those with ticks in their coats), should be bathed a few days before the show, as the ticks (small areas of coloured hair); are very evident immediately after a bath. The coat may also be too soft immediately after bathing taking a day or two to return to its harsher condition. During the height of the show season there is no need to bath every time – a sponge down of the marked areas such as the hocks and feet and a rub with a damp towel can be very effective. After bathing and while the coat is still slightly damp, it can be powdered with chalk, cornflower, bleached fuller's earth or whatever else you favour. This will keep the coat clean until the day of the show and brushing it out before the show will take out any marks the dog may have acquired in the interim.

The latest Kennel Club directive has banned the use of block chalk or any other similar substance within the precincts of the show and any used in preparing the exhibit beforehand must be removed from the coat before entering the show. This means that you cannot use block chalk to clean up your exhibit on arrival. The Kennel Club is endeavouring to 'clean up' the showgrounds and to eliminate the clouds of chalk dust that formerly could be seen around the benches of those breeds that used it. The threat of being banned from the show-ring now hangs over anyone who cleans or beautifies their exhibit with such a substance. It is not a new problem. It is recorded that at the end of last century, the intense white so often seen around the show-ring was from the application of powdered chalk.

**Eyes and Ears**   Once your dog has been cleaned or bathed it is time to see to the details. Eyes should be avoided during actual bathing, and they should be bathed separately with cotton wool dipped in warm water to remove any mucus that may have accumulated. Ears should be kept clean at all times with a cleansing solution available from pet stores and veterinary surgeries. The edge of the ear-flaps can be softened with liquid paraffin or any lanolin-based cream and once softened the gritty dust gently rubbed off. If rubbed without first softening the hair will come away also.

**Teeth**   Teeth should be checked regularly, partly as training for the dog to become used to having his teeth examined both in the ring and by the vet. Some owners can get their dogs to open their mouths so wide that the back teeth and throat can be inspected whenever required. Teeth can be cleaned with any proprietary brand of toothpaste and a brush – most dogs enjoy the peppermint flavour! If the teeth are badly discoloured with tartar they may need to be scraped. Get the vet to show you how to do this for the first time and then you can scrape them yourself in the future. Elderly dogs have a build-up of tartar which can only be moved this way. Regular hard tack – biscuits and nylon bone – keeps the teeth in good condition. Bones are excellent cleaning agents, but as mentioned earlier, Bull Terriers have such strong jaws that even the strongest of marrow-bones will chip, causing a hazard. If given, bones should be removed before they are cracked and shedding chips which might puncture the intestines if swallowed.

**Feet and Nails**   Feet should be checked for cuts and grazes and any tar or oil stains which can be removed with nail varnish remover. The nails should be kept trimmed throughout the dog's life – a check along the edges with your finger will tell you if there is anything to file down. Normally the centre two nails will be kept short by regular road work, but the two outside ones may need tidying up and the dew-claw will certainly need to be checked. These can curl right round in a circle and dig into the dog's leg if left unattended. By running your finger around them you can feel how sharp and long the point may be and clip or file them accordingly. Nail clippers are one of the many canine accessories that can be purchased from the trade stands at a show. In fact, you will be able to see various types of clippers. I favour the guillotine type, but I also have clippers for puppy nails.

**Whiskers and Tail Trimming**  A sharp but blunt-ended pair of scissors should be used for trimming the whiskers. Novices are always very sorrowful about the removal of their pet's whiskers, but they all agree how much better the dog looks without them. The tail should be neat and tapering. Hold the tail out level and then trim the underhair. Some people shave the hair underneath the tail close with a razor but others trim with a pair of scissors removing the straggling hair and tapering the tail gradually to the tip. The tip of the tail can be very bushy and untidy and needs to be tapered to a fine point. If you are wary of this, ask the breeder or an experienced exhibitor at a show to trim the tail for you and show you how it is done. Bull Terrier exhibitors are always ready to help a newcomer to the breed.

## *Advance Packing*

Once the exhibit is ready you can turn to the other preparations. You will need a show bag containing all the dog's requirements for the day. This really needs to be one bag or container so that everything is together. It can be packed in advance and should be cleaned and packed upon return, ready for the next time. It should include such things as a towel, tissues and wipes (for yourself), and a small bottle of mixed shampoo that you can dab on to any dirty mark on the dog.

A feeding bowl, food and a bottle of water saves a search for the water tap when first arriving at the showground. Treats, titbits or bribes, and toys for the dog should be packed, as should a collar and lead and a clean rug for the bench. A bench chain ensures that your Bull Terrier remains put when you turn your back to talk to friends. This needs to be a strong chain with a swivel clasp so that the animal does not almost hang himself when turning around on the bench. One dog, left attached to the bench ring by a leather lead and collar suddenly appeared by his owner's side minus his collar, and, on inspection, without the lead either – all the leather had been eaten down to the metal buckle and clasp!

An increasing number of exhibitors are using cages now to bench their dogs. Not only can the dog settle down in a familiar bed, but with a padlock on the door exhibitors feel that their Bull Terriers are a little more secure from the menace of dog stealing. Cruft's demands a 'bars only' type of bench cage so that visitors to the show may still view your dog even when tucked up for a sleep.

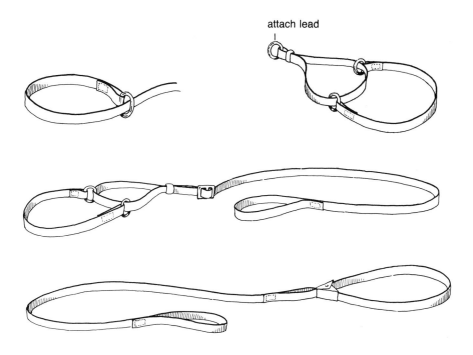

attach lead

Show leads.

A clean show lead should be packed. These can vary according to the type that you favour as the most efficient means of persuading your dog that he wishes to do the same as that which you have in mind! These leads are usually made of a flat, ribbed nylon and come in various widths. A half-inch (one-and-a-half-centimetre) width lead is the best for a puppy as it does not detract from the puppy's structure. There are three basic types of show lead.

1   A simple lead with a ring on the end which is used as a slip lead. This is useful particularly if the exhibit is well trained and knows how to stand and move in the ring. It can be instantly tightened if the need should arise, but can also be left loose resting on the lower part of the dog's neck or on his shoulders showing the dog's front, neck and shoulders to their best advantage.
2   The second is a martingale type, which is very useful for the stronger and more wilful animal. It consists of collar, adjustable loop and lead all in one. They can be bought in several sizes of loop as well as width and should be purchased with a particular dog in mind. If the collar is too big the dog will slip out.

Slip ring on white nylon rope show lead.

3   The third type is a collar and slip clip that can be adjusted to fit your dog. This can occasionally let you down in that the clip becomes loose and no longer holds the collar at the adjusted width.

There are alternative white show leads available such as a rope or a white rounded leather lead, so there is plenty of choice to suit your own preference. One point to remember is that white Bull Terriers are always shown on white show leads. An ordinary leather collar and lead make the Bull Terrier look heavy and tough, but in no way enhance structure or movement. It is not advisable to glamorise your exhibit to the extent of presenting him in the ring in a red or blue collar or lead – a Bull Terrier needs to display his virtures and does not require a brightly coloured collar cutting the line of his long neck. If you do not have a white show lead they can be bought at most of the Bull Terrier Club Shows or at the large pet supply stands at the larger General Championship Shows but they are not often available in your local pet shop.

You will also require some means of attaching your ring number to your jacket. Some people use their club badge or a Bull Terrier

A good collar like this one will show your dog's neck to best advantage.

brooch. There is, however, a very efficient number clip which is available at most shows. This is a pin which the exhibitor uses to display the ring number of the exhibit. They sell very cheaply at most shows and are easily mislaid, particularly when readily lent to fellow exhibitors or dropped to the bottom of one of your many pockets, so it is best to have two or three in your show bag.

## Personal Requirements

Any refreshments, cold drinks or the thermos flask should be put out to remind you to take them with you. A little time devoted to your personal requirements will pay dividends. Work out a suitable wardrobe – weatherproof if it is to be an outdoor show. Wear garments with plenty of pockets for your money, cheque book, credit cards and valuables. Ladies too – many a handbag has been taken from a bench. Ladies should also consider the length of their skirt. There is a lot of bending to do when handling a dog in the ring! Flat or low-heeled shoes are a must. A considerable amount of time is spent standing around, waiting to go into the ring and then once in the ring it would be difficult to walk at the speed required to show your dog's movement to its best advantage if you were tottering on high heels, or if the heels of your shoes kept sinking into the soft turf of the outdoor ring. You will also require either pockets or a pouch-type apron to contain all the treats, titbits and toys to entice your exhibit to stand to attention in the ring.

Having gathered everything together for the dog's day out, spare a little time to check over the car. After all these preparations it would be very disappointing to break down or run out of petrol and be too late for your class. Prepare the dog's bed and put in a spare dog rug (in case he proves to be a poor traveller), and a plastic bag for any soiled bedding might be a wise precaution.

# 8

# At The Show

## The Showground

Let's take a trip to a General Championship Benched Show first of all, as on the whole the Open Shows and the breed club shows work on the same principles.

Having carefully displayed your car-park sticker, you hopefully will have been guided to the correct car-park, nearest to the entrance of the showground for Bull Terriers. With efficiency, you will have timed the journey well to give yourself half an hour to unwind leisurely before moving on to the rest of the day. Coffee and a snack to start with, while you watch the other cars being parked tightly alongside yours and all shapes and sizes of canine exhibits and their owners disgorging from them. The accompanying paraphernalia is amazing. Trolleys are loaded up with cages, grooming equipment, blankets and bags, and the dog as well, for whom all this is considered essential! Then the procession leads off towards the entrance gate.

When all is reasonably quiet in your immediate vicinity, then is the time to remove Bull Terriers from their travelling cages and take them for a brief walk. Having then gathered up your requirements it is your turn to join the route march to the show. This can be the most hazardous part of your journey so far, as not all car-parks have neat asphalt roadways for your dog to march along (although those held on County Agricultural Show sites are usually well equipped). More often the car-park is a field made into a mud patch by recent rains, often of a gloriously staining hue – remember the famous red earth of some parts of Great Britain. If this is the third or fourth day of a General Championship Show the whole place will be well churned over. A Border Terrier can be tucked under an arm, so possibly could a Miniature Bull Terrier, but a 70–80 lb (31–36 kg) Standard Bull Terrier cannot. Occasionally, breeders and exhibitors resort to the cage-on-trolley system adopted by such breeds as the

At the show.

West Highland Whites, but it needs to be a very strong trolley with an exceptionally good set of wheels to cope with the weight of a dog and the uneven and often soggy ground. Bull Terriers are notoriously messy when they know you wish to keep them clean. It is not only their feet and hocks that could be stained, but the whole of the undercarriage could become splashed and grubby. In the past the dog would have been chalked after his bath and the white areas of the coat would have been protected from the mud, but now that chalk has to be completely removed before entering the precincts of the show, it is only of limited assistance here. Let us hope for a show season of sunshine and dry ground, otherwise we shall have to resort to considerable bench bathing to restore our exhibits for presentation to the judge.

One word of warning – on leaving the car do not leave any other dog in the car without sufficient ventilation. If you have ever been in a traffic jam on a hot day you will know how quickly a car can become hot and airless. Most larger shows make arrangements for dogs not entered in the show to be cared for in a separate marquee at the entrance gate. Check that the car is securely locked as dog thieves will be on the prowl and show personnel cannot take responsibility for your dogs however vigilant they may be. Finally, make a note of some landmark by which you can locate your car on

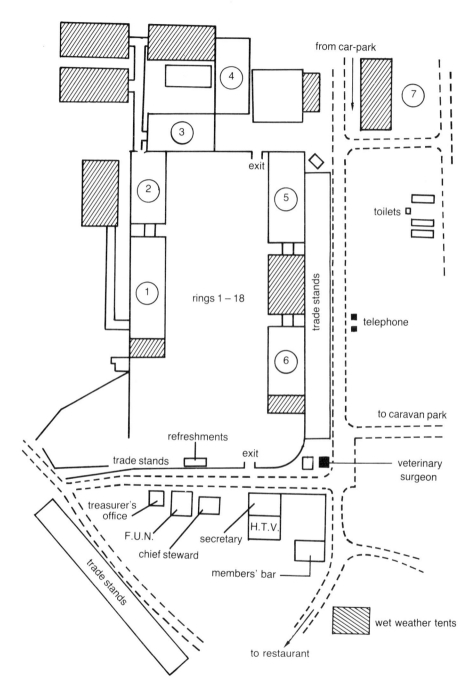

Show ground-plan.

your return. It is suprising how difficult this can be when on leaving the show you find the number of cars has multiplied in all direc tions. Bull Terriers often have a remarkable homing instinct and should you be lost you might as well let him have a go at leading you to the car.

On entering the showground gate attendants will check your passes or admission tickets, others will be in charge of catalogue sales and yet more will direct you in the general direction of your benching marquee. White Bull Terriers are easy to spot in a crowd and you can occasionally find one ahead of you to follow. Each tent is numbered in case you have been calmly strolling along consulting the plan displayed in the catalogue, and outside each marquee is a list of the breeds that are benched therein. You may enter the tent at the opposite end from the Bull Terrier section and then have to guide your exhibit down an aisle between rows of excited, vocifer ous benched dogs without a Bull Terrier in sight. Eventually a familiar face will come into focus and you will almost be there.

The way to avoid all these antics is to have a friend or partner with you who will go ahead while you wait outside with the dog and who will locate the bench, leave his share of the luggage on it and return for you. Alternatively, leave your dog in the car while you establish yourself on the bench and then return for him when he can enjoy your full attention all the way to his bench. There are arrange ments at the gate for you to pass in and out in this fashion. It is only the dog who once in, must not leave again until the stipulated time and with the relevant exit document.

Your show pass will have the dog's bench number on it. If you have entered two dogs of the same breed they will be benched next to each other. Ensure that you put the dog's exit pass somewhere secure in order to be able to get the dog out of the show afterwards. Once you reach the bench, the dog can be settled on to his rug and chained with the swivel bench chain to the ring provided, or made comfortable in his cage. These cages are becoming more prevalent at shows now, with the disturbing number of thefts being reported. Your dog is safe from passers-by and is far less likely to work himself up into a nervous frenzy, particularly if he is accustomed to short periods in a cage at home, where he has been able to chew his bone without interference or have a peaceful nap. You too will be more relaxed in the knowledge that all and sundry are not attemp ting to pat your dog when he is clean and groomed for the ring. Should there be an elegant bitch on the ajacent bench, your dog may

The benches.

well do his best to get a little nearer. Two dogs can make a remarkable noise in their vying for a lady's attention. Watch the bench behind, as it may harbour another breed – maybe one of your dog's pet hates.

Once he is settled and has been offered a drink of water you can attend to such matters as locating the ring for your breed, finding the ring entrance and the route with the least number of obstacles from bench to ring. Remember to check the starting time for your breed. In theory, the benching arrangements are near to your ring, but occasionally this is impossible. The rings are roped-off areas in the middle of the showground, surrounded by the marquees and the various trade stands. Some tents will be those of the officials, judges, stewards, the Show Manager, the Show Secretary and the veterinary surgeon's quarters.

The main ring will be larger than the surrounding rings, often distinguished by low fencing, decorative floral, or shrub displays and podiums for the Best in Show and other such prestigious winners. It is here that the winners from each breed are invited to compete for the Group, in our case for the Best Terrier in the show. There will be gangways separating the other rings and a few seats or

101

An indoor show.

benches lining the rings on two sides for spectators. Wet weather rings can be found marked out in marquees, or else at the end of the benching marquees, to be used by the relevant breeds within that marquee. These are small and the light is poor, and the larger breeds, including Bull Terriers, prefer to show outside if at all possible.

Arrangements at indoor shows vary a little from these outdoor shows as the large halls used will be divided into rings, either with ropes or with lines of spectators' chairs, and then avenues of benches will be erected in various parts of the hall, being as near to the ring for that breed as is possible. Smaller shows, Championship, Open or Limit, for a particular breed only, have one ring and often have permission from the Kennel Club to run an unbenched show.

Once the geographical locations have been sorted out, the next task is to check the catalogue and see that your entry is in order, the particulars are correct and that you are entered in the right classes. If anything is amiss make your way to the Honorary Secretary's office, as what may seem to you as a gross inaccuracy may be quite easily rectified. Next check your dog over. Give him a good brushing and remove any scuff marks or muddy patches. Check that his whiskers and tail are trimmed neatly, clean his nails (a spot of corn oil will do this job nicely), and dab a little corn oil on his nose, as this will make him lick it off and give him a moist, healthy-looking nose. Then settle him back on his bench with a few biscuits and a bowl of water until nearer the time for his class.

Now attend to yourself – a quick tidy up to remove those white dog hairs that get everywhere, clip on the ring number for the first of your exhibits, load up with the required enticements and check the show lead is untwisted and ready. If you have a long wait until your breed is required in the ring, you might want to go shopping at one of the many stands that are displaying their wares, particularly if you are in need of some commodity that is likely to be in great demand. You can also obtain supplies of the various dog foods, vitamins, drinking bowls and show paraphernalia that are often unobtainable from the local pet shop. However, you should have a friend or partner with you who can stay with the dog, or else make arrangements with one of your benching neighbours to keep an eye on your dog while you are away – dog theives only take a few seconds, often in full view of, and watched by, other exhibitors who do not realise that the people removing the animal are not the dog's owners.

Many exhibitors leave their purchases until the day's work in the ring is over and they then walk their dog with them for a brief visit around the show amenities. The dog must not leave the bench for more than fifteen minutes at a time for exercise purposes, but many shows allow dogs to leave once they have been judged. It is only when a large part of the revenue is anticipated from spectators that there is a time span before which one cannot leave with the exhibits. This is to ensure that visitors walking around the breed benches have something to see. However, most shows recognise that prime consideration should go to the dogs and exhibitors who may have left home at 4.00 a.m. would really like to be on their way home as soon as possible. After all, without the exhibits and exhibitors there would be no dog show.

## Bull Terriers in the Ring

When the Bull Terrier breed is to be in the ring make sure you are there in plenty of time. It is discourteous to keep a judge waiting and there are enough hidden problems without arriving at the ring

Bull Terriers in the ring.

in a flustered state and having to scramble to the only remaining space in the line, dragging your dog behind you. If you are not in the first couple of classes (often Minor Puppy and Puppy Dog) then watch the class carefully and discover where the stewards are placing the new entries. Dogs from the concluded class will be placed down one side of the ring in the order of their wins, the new entries down another. Observe the judging procedure and look for what this particular judge expects of you and of your exhibit.

Your ring number may have been posted to you with your admission pass, or it may have been ready for you on your bench when you arrived. At other shows (usually the unbenched shows), the ring steward will hand out the ring numbers as soon as he has called the class into the ring. It helps if you have noted your ring number from the catalogue and can quote it to the steward. Once acquired, use your number clip or a pin to display your ring number clearly so that the judge and steward can readily identify which dogs have come into the ring and which dogs have won the class.

Most judges are very lenient towards a wayward exhibit, giving you every opportunity to show the dog, particularly at Open

Shows, but at big Championship Shows a judge will expect that exhibitors know how to handle and show their dogs. With large classes it is impossible for any judge to allow time for untrained exhibits. A dog show is planned on the basis of a judging time of three minutes per dog and you have a lot to pack into that three minutes. However, the dog should be on show the whole time that he is in the ring. The judge will continually be making mental notes of his stance and rank placing. He should come into the ring unafraid and eager to show himself off, giving the judge every opportunity to assess his good qualities.

The judge will commence by looking down both rows of dogs and will then call each exhibit in turn to the centre of the ring. He will survey the dog from a distance, standing back to get an all-over impression, and walking around the dog to view him from all angles, noting the balance of head, neck, placement of shoulders, proportion of back and loin, quarters, tail set and so on before coming up to the dog for a closer inspection of the eyes, mouth, teeth and ears. Your Bull Terrier should stand to attention, looking alert and as intelligent as possible. Your home training should now prove its worth as you keep the dog's attention on your hand and the possibility of a titbit reward rather than allowing him to fidget and turn round in an effort to see the judge. The judge will ask you the age of the Bull Terrier as a means of introducing himself to you and the dog, before touching the dog and feeling his bone structure. You will be asked to show the judge the dog's mouth – infinitely preferable to the judge opening the mouth himself, as he may inadvertently pass germs from dog to dog. You need to peel up the lips so that the teeth and jaws can be inspected, but remember it is the judge who wants to see inside – it is not necessary for you to be peering in as well, other than to ensure that the teeth are visible. Many a struggle ensues when a Bull Terrier finds himself with two faces in close proximity.

After all this it will be time to show the judge how well your Bull Terrier can move. The size of the ring usually determines the pattern you will be required to follow. Sometimes you walk in a straight line up and down the centre of the ring while the judge views the movement from front and behind. He will then move down the ring to gain a side view of the movement as you repeat the performance. If the space permits, then the pattern could well be a triangle – proceeding down one side of the ring, across the bottom of the ring and diagonally back up to the beginning. This is quite

Judge, Mrs C. Larkin inspecting teeth. Note that it is the owner who handles the dog.

tricky at the corners and you should make sure that the dog is on your left-hand side, so that he is nearest to the judge and that you are not blocking the judge's view of the dog. If all the attention goes to the dog's head and he decides to show off by pacing or by bounding and leaping around, stop him, return to the beginning of that section of the route and calm him down before starting off again.

Once all the new dogs have been seen by the judge, the dogs carried forward from the previous class will be reconsidered and eventually the judge will make his decision and as per Kennel Club rules will place the dogs from left to right down to fourth or even fifth place. If you are one of the fortunate ones and have been picked out, then you should wait in line until the judge has finished making his notes about the exhibits and you have been presented with your rosette or place card. If you are among the less fortunate, the steward will dismiss you and you may leave the ring or move across to join the 'seen' dogs if you are going forward to the next class. Then the procedure starts all over again.

Once your classes are completed you can relax, unless of course this is your day, you were placed first and therefore need to go back into the ring to compete against the other unbeaten dogs for the Best Dog or even the Best of Breed. The steward will let you know if you are required again. Otherwise, put the dog back on his bench, give

The show pose.

him a drink and offer him a light meal, and let him settle down to a peaceful sleep. You can now relax until it is time to remove your dog and start the journey home. You may be able to return to the ringside and watch the rest of the competition or to watch some other breeds going through their paces. However, make sure someone back at the benches is keeping a check on your dog. Many Bull Terrier owners take it in turns to watch the benches, to ensure that the dogs are secure from theft and any other antics.

If you have entered any other classes such as Any Variety Puppy or a Special Stakes class you will need to find out when and where these are to be held. Then your Bull Terrier will need tidying up after his sleep and exercising so that he is full of enthusiasm for his return visit to the centre of attention. If your breed classes commenced later in the day it could mean a run from your ring to the variety classes which might even have started before your own breed classes have finished. If this is the case, send a message to the ring steward to ask if you may join the class as soon as is possible. Officially, you can no longer join such a class later than ten minutes after it has started.

So much for the large General Championship Shows. Let us now look at Open and Limit Shows run by the breed clubs, catering only for fanciers of their breed. Arrangements are much the same as for the General Championship Shows but on a smaller scale. Often the organisers have been granted permission by the Kennel Club to run an unbenched show and therefore you may not be sent a ring number and admission pass in advance. To ensure that your entry has been received you can enclose a stamped self-addressed post-card which can be returned to you as proof that your entry has been received.

Once you have arrived at the show you may need to use your car as your main base, keeping the dog there until you wish to take him into the hall or showground. The main difference is that you can take your dog in and out of the precincts of the show as often as you like provided he is entered in the show. You can walk him into the hall to acclimatise him to the indoor atmosphere and noise and then take him out for a walk or back to the car to groom him for the ring.

The main hazard to be aware of is that of a highly polished floor. Whether at a canine society show catering for many breeds in a leisure centre or a small hall hired for a breed club Limit Show, a polished floor is dangerous. Bull Terriers simply hate to have insecure footing. Once they realise that they are inclined to slip on the polished surface, they go even sillier and try a spread eagle act. Once they start slithering around they are liable to strain a tendon or worse.

The show-ring itself will either be covered with tarpaulin, or will have wide strips of rubber matting laid out where the dogs are to stand and walk. Remember, however, that it is for the dogs not the exhibitors. Some clubs have wide enough matting for both dogs and handlers to move on, but often a handler can be seen marching down the middle of the matting while the poor Bull Terrier has to manage as well as possible with one foot on the matting and one on the wooden floor – hardly the best way to display his rear action! One other hazard in an indoor arena is that of the other dogs waiting for their turn. The ring will most likely be surrounded by two rows of chairs and although dogs are not allowed to sit at the ringside, they can be with their owners in the second row. A determined Bull Terrier is quite capable of wriggling under the front row of seats towards the ring and from there making very taunting remarks to your dog while he is doing his best to please you and the

Parade of Champions: Ch. Cousin Charlie of Hollyfir – a
superb head with a good mouth, excellent front and neck and
a short back.

Ch. Ajestaweek Star Jester – a well-balanced dog of excellent construction.

110

Ch. Ghabar Dee Jay – a beautiful bitch of perfect temperament.

Ch. Ghabar Silver Sea – the latest Ghabar Champion at sixteen months. Good confirmation with an admirable head.

judge. If this happens, move a little further down the ring where you and your dog can concentrate on the matter in hand.

Club shows have far more trophies and cups to be awarded than the General Championship Shows, such as Best Puppy, Best Novice, Best White Bull Terrier handled by a Lady Exhibitor, a Member's Only Trophy, Best Coloured Dog and another for the Best Coloured Bitch and so on. The steward will let you know if you may be needed later in the day to compete for any of these. Somewhere near the officials' table will be a board where the results of each class are pasted up so that you can mark up your catalogue with the winning dogs for future reference when you are at home. There will also be a book for you to sign should you be the proud winner of a trophy, so that the Secretary knows where the trophy is going for the year, or maybe only until the next show.

On returning home from a show it is a good practice to change all your top clothing and shoes and to wash your Bull Terrier's feet before letting him mix with any other dogs in your household. This may seem over-cautious but prevention is better than cure. Your show dogs may be up to date with their injections but what about those you left at home and the neighbour's pets? Finally, do not forget to fill in your records of the show, particularly with any wins and points you may have gained towards your Junior Warrant. I also have a column for a note of the time it took to travel to the show for reference when it is time to repeat the performance next year.

# Judging Bull Terriers

The organisers of the show will provide each judge with a judging book which will have the exhibit numbers of the dogs entered in each class listed, and tear-off strips for the results. The judge has to judge the classes in the order in which they are entered in the judging book. The judge's award is final unless a genuine mistake has been made. He is able to withold an award for any reason. He is not allowed to make any public commentary whilst judging, though many exhibitors do like to talk to the judge after the show is over for his opinion regarding their exhibit.

There are two types of judge – the breed specialist and the all-rounder judge. Thirty or more years ago judges came out of those who had worked their way through large kennels, working with many breeds and as many as three hundred animals at any one time. Many eminent judges and people in the dog world started this way, but nowadays it is no longer possible. Very large kennels ceased to exist after the Second World War and today the breed judge will probably be an expert breeder and exhibitor in his own breed. He will have moved slowly into judging, first the small Open Shows and then the breed club shows before gaining Championship Show status by being approved by the Kennel Club to award Challenge Certificates. He will compare the Bull Terrier exhibit feature by feature with the Standard and will be able to assess the overall balance of the animal, looking also for quality and type. The all-rounder judge is more likely to be judging the animal as a whole, looking for quality and type rather than individual breed features.

Bull Terriers are judged to their Breed Standard. It is important to remember that one dog is not judged directly against another. Otherwise how could different breeds possibly be judged together, other than on health and showmanship? Each Bull Terrier is compared point by point with the Bull Terrier Breed Standard and then is compared with other dogs in the class. It is important therfore for the judge to be fully familiar with the Standard, the type and the quality expected of a Bull Terrier. In Great Britain, white and coloured Bull Terriers compete in the same class – apart from at the Coloured Bull Terrier Club's annual show. In some other countries, however, there are separate classes for white Bull Terriers and coloured Bull Terriers. Standards in various countries tend to differ and a foreign judge should familiarise himself with the Standard for that country before entering a ring. For example, great stress is laid upon the dog possessing the correct number of teeth in some countries and a judge must remember to count the teeth when examining a Bull Terrier in such a country.

A judge will first of all assess the quality of the entire class. All-rounder judges ask the exhibitors to take their dogs round in a circle. This is very unpopular with Bull Terrier exhibitors as it merely upsets the dogs. The rings are far too small for a dog who naturally hates to be followed by a potential adversary, and who has been blessed with eyes which keep him aware of a possible attack from the rear. Very few Bull Terriers will do themselves credit during this type of exercise despite hours of practice at home. There is not space to show the drive in his movement and with his head down pulling towards the dog in the front he is hardly likely to be able to be assessed for balance. The exhibitor then has to settle him back into his show behaviour again. They should be trained to this particular practice ready for the day when they go forward to represent the breed in the Group class, but when that day comes it invariably seems as if your Bull Terrier knows he is the tops and will be only too happy to show himself off to the inferiors around him!

The judge will then call each dog out in turn for individual inspection. He should take care not to come between the handler and the dog as this is an invasion of the dog and handler's space and may be grounds for canine objection! The judge will feel the dog to assess his various points of structure and in the case of a dog will check that he has two fully-descended testicles. (Remember, to be a monorchid is not a fault in Great Britain, though it may be in some other countries.) The mouth then needs to be inspected, and the judge will ask the handler to show him the teeth. The judge should help only if the handler is unable to manage to hold the dog quietly enough for the teeth and jaws to be properly inspected. When it comes to assessing movement, the judge should watch from behind and in front as the dog moves away and then back towards him. He should then move to the side of the ring in order to assess the stride and drive from the side of the dog.

After taking another look at the entire class, including those carried forward from previous classes, the judge will choose his winner. Having previously checked on how many place cards are to be presented, he will pick out as many dogs. If this means that only one competitor is left unselected he may courteously ask him to take up the fifth or sixth place. The judge may dismiss any others not chosen, and then fill out his Judging Book making notes on his choice of winners. They should wait in their positions showing their dogs to their best advantage until he has completed the notes ready for his critique.

When he calls for all unbeaten dogs and any others he may wish to invite back, he will select Best Dog, write up his notes and sign the Challenge or Reserve Challenge Certificate. Finally, he will select Best Bitch and Best of Breed. A good judge needs to be courteous towards the exhibitors who have done him the honour of showing under him. He should have quiet but efficient confidence and be able to make a firm unbiased decision, based upon knowledge and experience.

# System of Awards

As there are many more exhibitors and dogs than there are awards, it is really only worth participating in the show game if you are going to treat it as your hobby (unless of course you are professionally involved). Pleasure is gained by the owner from showing a handsome Bull Terrier in peak condition, that is a credit to his upbringing. It is an added bonus when you find that your dog is as good as and even better than the others in the class.

Each show provides place cards to fourth or fifth place. In Great Britain they are coloured red for first place, blue for second, yellow for third, and green, purple or any other hue for fourth, fifth or Very Highly Commended. In America, first place is blue, second is red, third is yellow and the fourth is white. After the class awards come the awards for Best Puppy, for which the Best Puppy Dog, Best Puppy Bitch and Best Novice compete. At the end of the dog classes, and again after the bitch classes the competitions for Best Dog and Best Bitch can take place. If this is a Championship Show the judge can also award a Challenge Certificate to the winners should he think they are of sufficiently high standard to be worthy of the title of Champion. The winner in each sex may receive a Challenge Certificate and the runner-up in each sex a Reserve Challenge Certificate. The judge may withold these honours if he feels the standard of exhibits on that day does not warrant them.

In the various regional Bull Terrier clubs, there are other trophy and cup competitions. These are advertised in their schedule. Often the competitors have to qualify on a point system of wins gained at shows held by that particular breed club, or else they may be invited to compete. The most prestigious awards are those competed for annually at the Bull Terrier Club Trophy Show. These are the Regent Trophy, the Ormandy Jug for Dogs and the Ormandy Jug for Bitches. The Bull Terrier Club Committee appoints a panel of experts to select competitors from the dogs and bitches that have entered Championship Show competitions during the last twelve months. The Regent Trophy is for dogs or bitches shown for the first time at Championship level during the past twelve months, and is similarly selected. Although there is only one year in which you may be selected for the Regent Trophy, you may be able to enter for the Ormandy Jugs twice where you can be amongst far more mature company.

115

The American scene is rather different, as there champions gain their honours through a points system. To become a champion, the dog needs to win fifteen points, which are awarded only in the winners' class, and can vary from one to five points according to the show. Some countries use the American points system to select their champions, others use the British system or an amalgam of both. On the whole it is considered easier to select champions under the points system as once chosen, they leave the field free for newcomers. Bull Terriers have an unspoken code by which they retire from the ring once they have been made a champion, showing only at the Bull Terrier Club Championship Show and at Cruft's. This used to mean that many champions were not seen again once they had gained their title, and become handsome mature animals. However, there is now a new trophy available – the Ramond Oppenheimer Memorial Trophy – one for Best Dog and another for Best Bitch. These are very handsome claret jugs and are awarded on a points system based on a maximum of five Challenge Certificates. Thus, we may now see far more champions in the Open classes at Championship Shows.

The Kennel Club issues a Junior Warrant to any dog that has obtained twenty-five points before the age of eighteen months. For each first prize in a Bull Terrier class at a Championship Show three points are awarded and one point for each first prize awarded in a Bull Terrier class at an Open Show. It also requires show win qualifications for the dog or bitch to be entered in the stud-book. These are the winning of a Challenge Certificate, Reserve Challenge Certificate or first, second or third prizes in Open or Limit classes at Championship Shows. Entry in the stud-book is sometimes one of the qualifications for Cruft's Dog Show.

# 9

# Breeding and Mating

Most breeders point out that dog breeding is a fascinating hobby but not a profitable one, and then they proceed to outline the financial burden undertaken when you launch forth on a breeding programme. Obviously commercial breeders must have a viable income, but when breeding dogs is purely a hobby should we really be swayed by financial considerations? If this is your main concern then I plead with you to turn your attention to some other hobby, or at least to a different breed of dog.

A Bull Terrier averages four in a litter. One hears of owners who are unable to attend shows because they are rearing a litter of nine pups, but this is unusual. In no way can small litters of three or four puppies be considered financially rewarding. No sooner will you have sold one puppy, than the electricity bill for the heating of the kennels will arrive! Even those who have tried to keep accounts for one particular litter have come up against difficulties. Each litter varies so much in its demands. How do you put a price on time spent sitting by the whelping bed? Who would deny an extra comfort to the bitch just because it had not been provided for in the planned budget?

Occasionally someone will deliberately set up a kennel in order to breed show stock. They will buy in a couple of bitches (the best show stock available at the time), and with the advice of their breeder will build up their own line. This is really the exception. Most of us start our breeding career already possessing a pet bitch and wanting some puppies. Apart from those who continually have false pregnancies, it is as well to rid oneself of the idea that it is good for bitches to have a litter. This is not necessarily true. It is really only an excuse, or an attempt to justify a desire to try your hand at rearing puppies or to acquire a show-stopping Bull Terrier of your own 'making'.

# Choice of Stud-Dog

Some research at an early stage can save much disappointment later. There is a saying that suggests you use the best dog available, but this should be qualified with the phrase 'for your bitch'. The Bull Terrier Club's Regent Trophy winner and the Ormandy Jug for Dogs winner each year are ensured of as much stud work as they can cope with, being the latest Bull Terrier dogs to hit the top show spot, but you should consider whether they are going to provide your bitch with what she is lacking. Look into any recessive genes which they might both be carrying by studying their pedigrees and by finding out all your can about their ancestors.

Genes are divided into two groups – dominant and recessive. They come from both parents. They can be carried dormant for several generations until they surface, having met a matching recessive gene from the other parent. In order to keep these genes dormant you should keep on breeding in the dominant qualities. Do not knowingly mate two Bull Terriers with the same faults unless it is the only way to gain a particular virtue not available from any other source. An outstanding dog with a fault can be used subject to the bitch not having the same fault in her line. Dominant genes can always be seen and therefore one knows what is being carried, but research into the ancestry is necessary to find out what the recessive genes might hold. Recessive genes produce such problems as cleft palate, deafness, timidity, eye and skin problems.

To begin with, the best advice can often be obtained from the breeder of your bitch providing they have been in the breed for some time and are not themselves recruits. A reliable breeder will advise you on the best available dogs for your bitch and your requirements for the progeny. Information gained this way will be confirmed by the stud-dog owner or he may advise you to use another dog. Try to understand the reasons for this – perhaps he knows that you would be doubling up on a recessive gene, or that you are hoping for brindle progeny which cannot be obtained by mating your white bitch to his white dog however much brindle they might be carrying. Reputable breeders have the well-being of the Bull Terrier breed at heart and their advice should be heeded.

Interbreeding is often favoured for strengthening the line, and dominant genes are mated together but only sound stock without any very bad traits should be used. Line breeding is the pattern to follow here. The bitch should be taken to the best son of her father or of her grandfather. Look at the bitch's pedigree, how she was bred, where her main virtues come from and then do your best to line breed to it. Take the example of Champion Souperlative Summer Queen, a good bitch and a superb mover behind. Bred by Mr Harry Langford, she was by Champion Beech House Snow Vision and was the dam to seven champions. Miss Weatherill mated her to Champion Phidgity Phlasher of Lenster who was also by Champion Beech House Snow Vision. This produced three male champions – Champion Souperlative Brinhead, Champion Ormandy Souperlative Chunky and Champion Ormandy Souperlative Princeling. This breeding of half-sister to half-brother is a well recognised and successful type of mating, but should be researched thoroughly beforehand to check that they are not carrying the same faults.

Out crosses are interesting and can bring out or reinforce some aspect that is weak in your bitch. However, this does tend to reveal

Line breeding: Ch. Ghabar Crusader, Regent Trophy and Ormandy Jug Winner . . .

hidden traits that were unknown to you. After one such out cross, a litter of whelps all of whom had cleft palates had to be destroyed. On more careful investigation it was discovered that the great-grandsire of the dam tended to produce progeny with cleft palates. In this particular instance the breeder had unwittingly doubled up on this fault. Complete out crosses are hard to find as you will find that most Bull Terriers are related if the search goes back far enough. After an out cross (generally in order to introduce a particular feature, such as colour or temperament), the progeny should then be line bred back to their own blood lines.

A novice breeder should be aiming for soundness and quality with good temperament. The colour must also be considered. At one time white Bull Terriers were only bred to other whites, and brindle dogs were not only out of favour but became few in number. It was then realised that the brindle factor acts as a reinforcement for the other colours. Nowadays white Bull Terriers can be seen carrying colour such as a red ear or a brindle eye-patch. The 'all white' Bull Terriers will usually have a few coloured hairs behind the ear. Others will be quite heavily 'ticked' with small clusters of coloured

. . . and his son Ch. Ghabar The Admiral . . .

120

. . . and his daughter Ch. Temptress Lolar of Ghabar.

hair in their undercoat. Most have skin spots though you may only
be aware of this when the dog is wet.

White Bull Terriers mated to whites can only produce white
progeny whatever colour they are carrying. White Bull Terriers are
coloured but with the colour suppressed, though it may appear in
progeny from a mixed colour mating. Brindle however can only be
produced if one of the pair carries the brindle factor. Reds, fawns
and tri-colours cannot produce brindle when mated together. They
need to be mated to brindles, black brindles or those whites carrying
brindle. Two coloureds mated together can produce several whites
amongst the litter. Occasionally, such a puppy will be deaf. The
genes need to come from both parent lines for this and recent
research has shown that the inner ear and the colour both form from
the same cell which may be the reason for the colour link. It is also
considered that many dogs are partially deaf, hearing at a differnt
pitch from their owners.

121

# Arrangements between Dog and Bitch Owners

Having whittled down the various stud-dogs to the one you would like to use on your bitch, the first stage is to make contact with the stud-dog owner to discuss the possible service. You should exchange pedigrees and information regarding the breeding, colour, size and temperament of your dogs. The stud-dog owner will then be able to advise you as to whether or not the dog you are considering would be able to give you what you require to further your particular line. At this time you can also give the dog owner some indication as to when you expect the bitch to come into season.

Contact the stud-dog owner as soon as the bitch comes into season to make final arrangements, calculating the day of the visit (approximately the fourteenth day, *see* page 130). To ensure that the correct time has been covered, two matings are the ideal arrangement. These should be more than forty-eight hours apart to give the best coverage as the dog's sperm will still be alive for the interim period. It is pointless to mate each day. If it is possible to board the bitch at the stud-dog's premises then a tiring car journey for the bitch will be avoided. When long distances and air flights are involved, bitches are sometimes left at the kennels to be whelped as well, but I feel that this makes the whole business of breeding dogs a calculated and not emotive event. Consider your reasons for wishing to breed and whether or not this is the best possible way of achieving your aim.

Enquiries regarding the stud-dog fee should be made during the preliminary contact with the owner, so that you are clear as to how much you will be expected to pay at the time of the first mating and whether a cheque is acceptable or not. This fee is for the service on that day. It is the custom for the fee to include a further mating within the same season should you require it. Should your bitch not have any results, most stud-dog owners will offer you a free service next season; however, this is not obligatory, being entirely up to the dog owner, and most certainly is not transferable to any other bitch. Incredible though this may seem, several dog owners have had instances where bitch owners consider it their right to receive a free service on a second occasion, and have asked for it to be with a different bitch. The few times when I have needed another attempt, I have offered to pay whatever is required – a small fee for the time and trouble taken by the stud-dog's kennels or for the difference between the original fee and that now being charged for the dog (fees go up in leaps and bounds when a dog becomes a champion). Only once was an extra fee accepted.

One point to remember is that the stud-dog owner must be informed within a few days of the date for whelping if no litter has arrived. Normally the bitch owner would be proudly letting the other party know what had happened, and no message would indicate trouble. Contact should be made out of courtesy. A few stud-dog owners will not offer a free service if this information has not been given within a set time. This is to avoid unscrupulous breeders claiming that there had not been any results, when really a litter had been born and subsequently died. Fortunately, these instances are few and far between, but it does happen and the stud-dog owner should be aware of it. If a dog or bitch have changed ownership the offer is no longer open. However, if the dog has been withdrawn from stud then an alternative dog is usually offered.

Once the mating has been completed the stud-dog owner will give you a receipt for the stud fee, a copy of the dog's pedigree and will sign your Kennel Club registration form, which should have been filled in with the name and details of both dog and bitch and the date of the mating, to confirm that the mating has taken place. Sometimes the stud-dog owner will ask for first choice of the puppies in the litter instead of a stud fee, but an agreement must be reached as to what should be done if the puppies do not survive or there is only one puppy. Occasionally, first and third puppies are to be given to the stud-dog owner. I do not like this system at all as a puppy will sell for two and a half times the stud fee. I prefer to suggest that I am paid the fee when a pup has been sold. I also arrange to have first refusal, so that I have the opportunity of buying one of my dog's progeny at the selling price, less the stud fee. However, I do insist on all such arrangements being written down and each member of the partnership having a copy duly signed. Thus any agreements are kept on a business level.

There are a great many people who breed Bull Terriers. They are fifth in the Terrier registrations at the Kennel Club and fifteenth in All-Breed rankings. However, only a limited number of breeders are known for their skill, expertise and experience at stud work. Many breeders, particularly novices, rely entirely on the stud-dog owner when it comes to mating their bitch.

# The Stud-Dog

Although the majority of dogs are capable of mating, a stud-dog is one who has been trained for the work. Ideally he is typical of the breed both anatomically and temperamentally. He should be used with discrimination as any hereditary faults that are being carried can be reproduced in the progeny. (Traits can be carried for four generations before revealing themselves.)

The bitch owner may have spent considerable time and care in selecting the stud-dog that he feels will do the most to improve his stock and to further the breed, so too the stud-dog owner needs to be selective as to which bitches he agrees to service. A poor litter can reflect badly on the stud-dog. If possible, the stud-dog should be recorded in the Kennel Club Stud Book – signifying that the dog's breed quality is sufficiently high to enable him to win and to reproduce winning stock. (Bitches too are registered in the Kennel Club Stud Book upon qualification.) The Stud Book register number can be displayed on the dog's stud card along with particulars of his breeding, date of birth, colour, weight, a photograph, the stud fee and owner details. His details can also be advertised in the canine press, including his Challenge Certificate or Reserve Challenge Certificate wins. Check that the correct terms are used in any advertisement – 'sire' for the dog and 'dam' for the bitch mother. Puppies are 'by' a certain sire and 'ex' or 'out of' a dam. Affixes are part of the Bull Terrier's Kennel Club registered name and must be included; they indicate the kennels and line from which the dog stems. Should the dog be the proud possessor of a title that too should be included.

# Care of the Stud-Dog

A strong virile stud-dog needs to be well looked after with a high protein diet including raw meat, fish, eggs and milk, added vitamins B and E, and adequate exercise to keep him in good condition. His coat should be kept clean and his nails trimmed and filed so that he does not mark the bitches during mating. No one wants a show bitch scarred down the sides of her body. He should have regular booster inoculations and his external organs ought to be checked for signs of infection or pus. The dog must be fertile and a proven sire.

```
┌─────────────────────────┐
│                         │
│                         │
│    space for photograph │
│                         │
│                         │
└─────────────────────────┘
```

Breed _____     Kennel Club No. _____

Sex _____       Date of Registration _____

Colour and Markings _____  Kennel Club Stud Bk. No. _____

_____            Owner _____

Date of Birth _____  Address _____

Breeder _____

Pedigree

| Parents | Grandparents | G. Grandparents |
|---------|--------------|-----------------|
| Sire    |              |                 |
|         |              |                 |
|         |              |                 |
|         |              |                 |
| Dam     |              |                 |
|         |              |                 |
|         |              |                 |
|         |              |                 |

I certify that this pedigree is correct to the best of my knowledge

signed _____ date _____

Stud card.

# Anatomy

The dog has two testicles contained in the scrotum which secrete the spermatozoa contained in seminal fluid and conduct them to the penis. This consists of erectile tissue with a fine pointed end at the front part and a bulbous enlargement at the other. There is also a small bone. The organ has a loose protective skin sheath – the prepuce. When mating, the erectile tissue becomes firm but it remains flexible, thus enabling the dog to penetrate the bitch and to later turn to face the opposite direction. The prepuce must have been pushed back beyond the bulb for a turn to be attempted – if not, turning will cause the dog great pain. Nerve impulses enable him to eject the fluid, and compression of the veins by the muscles near the bulb causes the bulb to become engorged with blood swelling up to five times its normal size.

It is this swelling within the female passage that causes the 'tie' as the female's structure is such that it can 'lock' around the swollen bulb. A tie need not take place for a mating to be successful as penetration is sufficient to cause ejaculation. Clear fluid is ejaculated first of all, followed soon after by the thicker white fluid containing sperm. This is pumped by rhythmical movements on the part of the dog and by the bitch's uterus. Following this is a clear alkaline fluid, usually while the pair are tied and the dog is turned. This state can be maintained for anything from two minutes to one hour, though usually it is a period of ten to thirty-five minutes. When copulation has been completed sperm will have travelled to the ovaries to fertilise the ova or egg cells. Should some of the last fluid be spilt on separation it is of little importance as it does not contain any sperm.

The scrotum has a lower temperature than that within the body, allowing the spermatozoa to thrive. No spermatozoa are produced if the testicles have not descended into the scrotal sac. Such dogs are known as cryptorchid or bilateral cryptorchid. A monorchid or unilateral cryptorchid is a dog with only one testicle descended, and fewer spermatozoa are able to live. Some monorchids are prolific sires, but the condition does reproduce itself in some of the progeny. In many countries it is regarded as a fault in the show-ring. An 'entire' or 'fully furnished' Bull Terrier has two normally descended testicles.

Over-use of a dog may result in a lower sperm count, but a period of rest usually restores the count. Although it does not necessarily determine the number of puppies in a litter it is advisable to use a

126

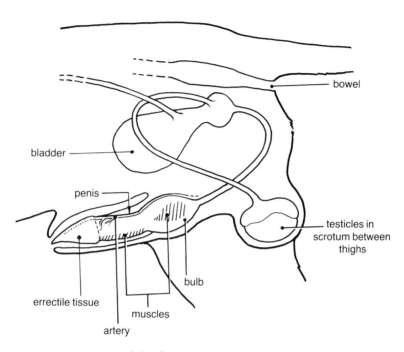

bowel

bladder

penis

testicles in
scrotum between
thighs

bulb

errectile tissue

muscles

artery

The reproductive organs of the dog.

young, virile dog to an older bitch and a young bitch to an elderly dog. The dog is responsible for the sex of the puppies, as it is the male who carries both male and female sex chromosomes. The best age to start a stud-dog working is ten months with a two-month interval between each service until he is eighteen months old. Over-use of a young stud-dog will weaken him.

Bitches often come into season together. Once the warmer weather arrives after a prolonged winter, bitches that had deferred their season during the cold days all require the attention of the stud-dog at the same time. This means more work than usual for the dog. After such seasonal work he must be rested for some weeks. Once one bitch has come into season in a kennel this will bring others in, one after the other. Three bitches can mean nine weeks of bitches in season in the kennel. Dogs will quickly become out of condition if left near bitches in season and they should be removed from the scene – into the house if possible, where they will stop pining and going off their food. A dog may howl when a bitch is in season which can set a whole kennel (dogs and bitches) off until some distraction can be found.

# The Brood Bitch

Bitches come into season, or 'on heat' at somewhere between five and a half months and nine months of age, and occasionally even later. Noting the various stages is very important. One of the earliest signs is that of the bitch needing to urinate far more frequently. She will pass a few drops at every possible stopping point when out on a walk. If a house dog she will want to visit the garden far more frequently than usual. I have also found over the years that most of my bitches are rather vociferous and even bad-tempered up to three weeks before they actually come into season. When I stop to consider why they are in such a mood, I usually discover that it is near the time for them to come into season.

The earliest visible sign is a swelling in the size of the vulva, gradually deepening in colour until eventually there are signs of a discharge. This too will deepen from a watery pink to a thick deep blood colour. This is known as the bitch 'showing colour' and is the time from which the calculations for the date of the mating can be made. Ovulation can last from nine to twenty-one or more days and needs to be recorded, even if the bitch is not to be mated on this occasion, as it adds to the information known about that particular bitch which will be very useful when it is her turn to be mated.

After a week or so the vulva becomes much softer and 'pouts', the discharge usually becoming faint pink after ten to fourteen days, and ultimately becoming colourless. During the early part of her season the bitch is not matable and owners should watch for signs of her becoming ready. She will begin to mix with the dogs, making her advances obvious by standing poised, with her hind parts towards any available dog. She will also curl her tail, lifting it out of the way of any possible action. The owner can tell if the bitch is ready by scratching her back at the root of her tail, and seeing if she curls it. If there is no dog on the premises she will do everything in her power to find one. More of the bitches on the Bull Terrier Club Lost or Stolen Register left home when in season than for any other reason. One particular bitch learnt to climb the wire mesh fencing of her run and then do a tight-rope walk along the top until she could jump down safely – luckily only into the paddock.

Throughout the bitch's season she has been giving off a delectable odour to all potential stud-dogs. Fortunately it is not detectable by people, but it does mean that there may well be callers at the front

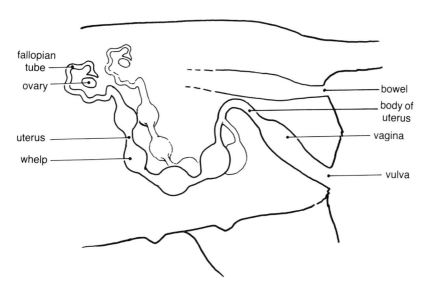

fallopian
tube
ovary

bowel
body of
uterus

uterus
vagina

whelp

vulva

The reproductive organs of the bitch.

Bitch with tail curled.

gate, the back door and anywhere they can get into the garden, just waiting for her to escape. There are several aerosol sprays on the market that I have found excellent, even if rather strongly perfumed. A quick spray on the bitch's rear parts before going for her walk will eliminate any inviting trail back to the house for aspiring young hopefuls. It would not be a sufficient deterent if you were to let her run free with the boys in the park, but it does put a stop to the annoying strays who hang around the gatepost in all weathers. (Spraying the gatepost can also be beneficial.) If it is possible, take the bitch some distance away by car before exercising her and there will be no trail for scent-seeking boyfriends to follow. Should she succeed in making contact with one of these roving dogs, then a trip to the vet's is the immediate course of action. He will give your bitch an injection to prevent conception. This is not a cure-all, as it can not be given too often.

This is a time for vigilance. Keep her safely indoors, in a secure garden or in a kennel and run. Do not put her outside in a shed or garage or any other unfamiliar place just because she may be 'drippy'. She needs extra love and fuss at such a time, not pushing out of sight somewhere strange to wonder what it is that she has done wrong.

The length of time that a bitch is willing to be mated varies between individual bitches – some for only a few hours, others for a week to ten days. Usually it is between two and six days, between the eleventh and fourteenth day, but the seventeenth and twenty-first have also been frequently successful. It must be noted that during this period and after a mating the bitch is more keen than ever to receive the attentions of a dog – any dog – and vigilance must be even greater. It has been known for a bitch to have a litter of fine Bull Terrier whelps only to have more a couple of days later who were of a very different parentage. In some cases the Bull Terrier mating has been too early and without result, but there is a pregnancy and a whelping – revealing whelps sporting curly coats and long wavy tails!

A bitch should not be mated at her first season if under twelve months. Her second season is a possibility if she is a mature bitch in every way – physically and temperamentally – though I prefer the third season. By this stage, she will be more capable of coping with the changes within her body, with her busy lifestyle when the whelps have arrived and will be more mentally stable when unfortunate events occur, such as a dead whelp or having to remove a deformed one. She is not a puppy producing machine and should be mated only every other season. That is one litter a year. There is a school of thought that a bitch of three or four years old before being mated will have a difficult time at whelping, but with adequate care during pregnancy and veterinary assistance on hand this need not be so. A bitch who has successfully raised litters may continue to do so until six or seven years of age, but no longer, as the progeny then is usually not of such quality as in the ealier years.

# The Mating

## *The Bitch*

If a maiden bitch, it is a good idea to visit the vet a few days before travelling to the stud-dog, to check that all is well and that there is no stricture present. If she is a bitch that has been mated but not had any successful results, the vet can give an injection to help events along, but there is a tight time schedule between the injection and the mating in order for it to be effective. Ideally the bitch will stay at the stud-dog's kennels, getting to know the chosen sire by being in an adjacent run. This is not often convenient these days, and the next best thing is for the bitch to be given light exercise on arrival to relieve herself and then, having had a good look around, meet the stud-dog. Neither bitch nor dog should have been fed before mating.

The bitch should be taken into the room first and allowed to sniff around and to calm down before the stud-dog handler brings in the dog. While remaining on the lead they can 'court' each other, usually chasing and circling around the room. In the wild, dogs would chase a bitch up to several miles, the fittest dog being the victor. In the confined space this may appear as the bitch trying to escape from the whole scene, but is usually only part of her flirting routine. She may appear aggressive towards the dog. This could well be no more than part of the act and she will calm down gradually, but if she is a highly-strung or aggressive bitch she may need to be muzzled to avoid marking the stud-dog.

## The Stud-Dog

Dogs have many idiosyncrasies at mating time and the stud-dog owner will have to be ready to accommodate them. However, it is generally recognised that the antics he gets up to on the first occasion will be his preferred method for evermore. This may explain why one particular dog that actually tied with a bitch in the nine-inch space underneath a dining-room sideboard was never encouraged to repeat the performance! One of his sons however was equally as idiosyncratic in that he steadfastly refused to attend a bitch indoors. He would escort her up to the lawn outside his kennel and entertain her in privacy. When handler and bitch owner discreetly peered around the corner to see why all was so quiet, he would roll his eyes with a look of disgust at the intrusion, and return his attention to the task in hand! This is known as natural mating. If indoors, breeders have been known to leave the room and watch through a window, returning only when it is time to assist by holding the bitch straight and steady, and then to turn the dog when the time comes.

At no time should the dog and bitch be left unattended. It would provide an opportunity for aggressiveness, risking injury to the dog and the bitch, or encouraging such a dislike of the situation that neither animal wishes to mate either now or on any other occasion. When two Bull Terriers of even temperament mate naturally the dog will take his time, pause and think about the situation, demonstrate affection and provided they are not hurried, the pair proceed to a normal, simple service. This calls on patient gentle encouragement from the handlers but in these days of long distance travel, the bitch owner is often anxious to be on the way home as soon as possible. The butch type of dog wastes no time on courting. He will mount immediately. If a dog is too aggressive he should be restrained as he could make a nervous bitch even more frightened. She may attempt to wriggle or roll over in order to get away. Both animals need patient reassurance to calm them down. A young novice may well go to the wrong end of the bitch. This is one of the reasons for taking a mature bitch to a novice dog – she will turn around and stand for him. He should be assisted at his first mating as he is learning what is expected of him. An experienced bitch will show him what to do. One visiting bitch made it very clear to my novice dog. She mounted him and went through rhythmic motions, then clambered off and wriggled underneath him.

A nervy dog, lacking in confidence, will not react positively to a responsive bitch. Here it is better to go straight into the routine described on page 134, watching for the attempts at penetration, immediately pressing the dog to the bitch and once there, holding him there. It is often better not to attempt to turn this type of dog, just hold him to the bitch throughout. I have had to keep a giant of a dog to a bitch with my knees while clasping him around his chest with my arms to hold some of his weight off the bitch who was rapidly sinking beneath him. Some dogs are not interested – a minority fortunately. With encouragement from the assistant, he can become an average, sound stud-dog, but he must not be rushed – once in three months for the first five or six services. All stud work needs patient handling. Very occasionally, hand stimulation may help – rub the penis gently, and when the erectile tissue responds, guide it to the vulva. However, some dogs object to interference. Always use an approving tone and talk to the dog by name. A harsh, impatient voice will discourage him. Remember he may have been scolded as a young pup or teenager for experimenting at the wrong time or place. Finally, if he is being very slow, threaten to take the bitch away, or even remove him for half an hour to cool his heels and think the situation over. This usually has the effect of making him very keen to come back to make sure she has not departed.

## Preparation of the Mating Room

The mating room should be as bare as possible – an empty garage, with good lighting and a window is best. There will need to be some form of heating for winter and a good latch on the door. I like a non-slip piece of carpet on the floor as I inevitably end up kneeling down there. A cushion, a couple of low stools and a higher chair will help to prepare for all eventualities and one or two doormats that can be used for the dog or bitch to stand on should either need to be raised slightly. You should have a jar of vaseline for the bitch, some disinfectant, in case you get scratched, a bandage in case the bitch should need to be muzzled, a bowl of drinking water (for the dogs) and a pair of thick leather gloves in case things get really rough!

# Method of Mating

It is advisable to have two people available to assist at a mating, each with a definite task to carry out. One should attend to the head of the bitch, the other to the opposite end and to the dog. The first handler should sit on a low stool, chair or upturned box of comfortable height for holding the bitch steady. The bitch should wear a strong leather collar which will not stretch allowing her to wriggle free. The handler should take a firm grip of the bitch's collar, one hand on either side of the neck. His job is to control the bitch and to keep her calm with soothing words. His main task is to restrain her impulse to swivel round. A scared bitch may attempt to run away, sit down, roll on the floor, or even attempt to bite the dog, all of which can be very discouraging to a young stud-dog. If the bitch does seem inclined to use her teeth, you may want to use a muzzle. The bitch can still move her lips and can give appreciative kisses to both the dog and the handler, but she has to keep her teeth to herself. If one is not available then the bandage mentioned in the list of equipment should be used to muzzle her. (*See* opposite.)

The second assistant can kneel on the floor or use a low stool. Having smeared the bitch's vulva with vaseline he then adjusts the height of the dog and the bitch by providing a mat for the lower animal to stand on. (The angle should not be horizontal as the steeper the angle the easier it will be for the dog to penetrate the bitch.) Once the dog has become enthusiastic to the task and tried to penetrate the bitch, the assistant should press the dog to the bitch and hold him firmly there. The bitch will very likely try to swivel round which causes the dog to slip out. The dog should take over but it is still useful to continue to hold him to the bitch, only relaxing when a tie has definitely been effected. Often the weight of the dog or the tendency to wriggle away, causes the bitch to sink slowly.

Difficult bitches can be aided by the second handler sitting on the ground or a low stool and stretching his legs out under the bitch, using his leg or knee to hold her up. If a third assistant is nearby, a linking of hands under the body of the bitch can also give support. One particular mating with a 75lb (35kg) dog and a smaller bitch found me in a very unorthodox position, applying pressure to the dog's rump with my shins and knees while I had my arms around his chest holding some of his weight off the bitch. This is not to be recommended for long ties, but at the time it worked well.

Sometimes the dog needs guiding to the bitch. It can save time

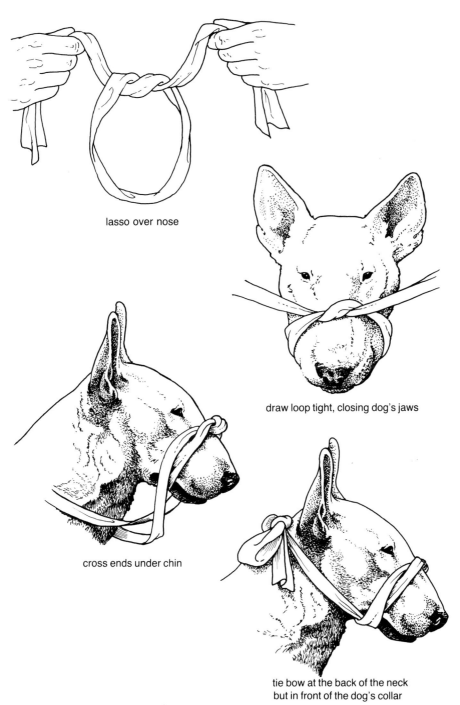

lasso over nose

draw loop tight, closing dog's jaws

cross ends under chin

tie bow at the back of the neck
but in front of the dog's collar

Using a bandage as a muzzle.

135

and energy. However, some dogs are completely put off by being handled, and you should take care. If the dog becomes fidgety and looks as if he might dismount before the bulb has swollen, he may slip out and if already tied he can injure himself and the bitch. He must be kept still until the tie has been securely achieved and he can be turned. To turn a dog once a tie has been satisfactorily achieved and there is no risk of him slipping out, the dog's front feet are guided to the ground on the right side of the bitch so that they are both standing side by side. The handler then gently steers the dog's left rear leg over the bitch's rear to her right – turning the dog to face the opposite direction from the bitch. This left foot is placed on the ground and the dog will move his feet slightly to the right. He is now standing in the same spot but facing the other way. By holding both tails together in one hand any pulling away is prevented, though as they prefer this position, both usually stand quietly at this stage.

Once copulation has been completed, both dog and bitch should rest. Check that the dog's penis has returned into its sheath. Until it has shrunk sufficiently to return, the dog will stand around looking uncomfortable. A gentle push on his chest to encourage him to take a step or two backwards often helps. If prolonged, the area can become dry, in which case a cloth wrung out in cold water may be gently applied or a dish of cool water held so that the whole exposed part can be dipped for a second or so. The penis will quickly contract and return to normal. Having been offered a drink, the dog is lead away to the quiet of his kennel and the bitch is taken to her kennel, cage or car to lie quietly. Care should be taken that she is lifted correctly (see page 141).

## Problems during Mating

If exploration is necessary, the assistant should check that the nail of his little finger is filed smooth, that he has scrubbed up with an antiseptic and smeared the finger with vaseline.

If the bitch has a narrow passage, penetration with a well vase-lined little finger can sometimes make it possible for a mating, but if too tight, veterinary assistance should be considered. A stricture or adhesion can be felt with the little finger as a hard obstruction. The bitch owner should take her to the vet as no mating will be possible. If a bitch is brought to the dog too late in her season the passage

136

may have tightened. Application of vaseline can occasionally massage and stimulate sufficiently for a service to be achieved.

In the case of either dog or bitch showing signs of fainting, a whiff of smelling-salts will usually cure them. It can be caused by the blood accumulating in the sex organs leaving only a limited supply for the brain.

Occasionally the stud-dog has a particular bitch in the kennel of whom he is particularly fond and he then refuses to show any interest in the visiting bitch. Another dog brought in to see the visitor sometimes makes the stud-dog sufficiently jealous but it is not a very advisable action where Bull Terriers are concerned. It is better to put the stud-dog away for half an hour to think it all out again. He will usually be sufficiently interested to want to see if she is still around.

# 10

# Care of the Pregnant Bitch

The bitch carries the whelps for sixty-three days. During this time she should be nursed carefully but not spoilt. This is a time when bitch and owner can develop a close bond culminating in her trust in you at the time of whelping. The care and attention you lavish on her should be backed with confidence developed from the know-ledge you have gained about your bitch's habits, likes and dislikes, and also the information you have gathered from other breeders and from authoratitive works on the events to come. Now, possibly more than at any other time, it is essential to remember that you are breeding Bull Terriers. They are not like any other breed when it comes to their antics in the whelping room.

Certainly gather advice on general whelping matters from what-ever source is available, but act primarily on that received from those with firsthand knowledge within the breed. No Bull Terrier Club Committee member will mind if you pump them for advice. The past President of the Bull Terrier Club, Mrs Sweeten, had someone phone from Scandinavia, frantic for help with an over-excited bitch whelping. Advice was clearly and calmly given and a later phone call confirmed all was now well. Do not be afraid of seeming incompetent. It is the Bull Terrier that is the main concern and Bull Terrier breeders recognise that each whelping can produce some aspect that has not been encountered previously.

## Signs of Pregnancy

Around the third week of pregnancy some breeders who know exactly where to feel along the bitch's abdomen, can find marble-like lumps. These increase and soften so that by the fifth week they are not so easily discernable. It is not advisable to prod a bitch – be patient and look for other signs. From the third week onwards the bitch's teats appear softer and gradually over the course of the

The brood bitch.

following three weeks they will steadily enlarge and the skin become much more pink. Between the fourth and fifth week the bitch will thicken and look tubby. One does not always feel certain at five weeks but you cannot possibly mistake her condition by six.

The most exciting time is when you feel the whelps moving for yourself. This is usually around the sixth or seventh week of pregnancy. When the bitch is asleep beside you on the sofa, if you rest your hand along her abdomen you will feel the future champions stir, turn over and in the later stages have a vigorous game of football. By this time you can see their movements as she lies basking in the sun or before the fire. During the last few days this movement will cease. Do not be alarmed, they are merely preparing themselves for their great adventure into the world.

# Diet

Appetites vary from bitch to bitch and on the whole you should trust her judgement. Meals need to contain plenty of body-building protein including meat, eggs, milk and fish, but the biscuit-meal and other starchy foods should not be increased. Brown bread and wholemeal biscuit will provide bulk without the fat. Watch for the greedy bitch, possibly asking for food as a means of seeking attention – titbits of little food value can fatten alarmingly. An increased diet should be given from five weeks onwards, splitting the meals in two if necessary. She should be given as much milk as she wants and water must always be available as she needs plenty of fluid to supply the water bags that surround the whelps. If giving a raw egg, then the yoke only should be used. Otherwise the whole of a cooked egg can be offered. During the last three weeks several small meals should be given as there is now less room for a large meal if the bitch is carrying rapidly growing whelps. Milk with glucose and uncooked egg yoke whipped together makes a nourishing snack to put down last thing at night. Take care that a lazy bitch, enjoying the extra attention does not become overweight as this will not help her at whelping time.

For those that have such tendencies, I cook plenty of vegetables to substitute for some of the biscuit meal. All the peelings from our own root vegetables, outer cabbage and other green leaves go into the pressure cooker to mix in with their meal. Raw sprouts, cabbage leaves and carrots are popular too, as are fresh apples and pears.

If the bitch goes off her food tempt her with special treats of liver, chicken and eggs, trying them raw or cooked. On the whole the bitch knows best what quantity she needs, but they do need to keep up their strength, and if she is refusing food it can be rather worrying as the time for whelping approaches. A particular fancy for sweet foodstuff of one pregnant bitch led me to dribble a little syrup over everything I offered her – even raw liver – and it was all gobbled down, having previously been refused. Sometimes, grated cheese sprinkled on top of an abandoned meal will make all the difference.

There are plenty of good proprietary brands of multi-vitamins for dogs available and vitamins A,B,D and E should be given. Cod-liver oil capsules are also recommended, but they can make the bitch's motions loose, so dose only to the recommended amount. Most important for Bull Terriers however is bone-meal, sprinkled on their food; some do not like it and will leave the dish, in which case it needs to be disguised, as it is essential for Bull Terriers to have strong heavy bones and these must be given a good start. Of vital importance for Bull Terriers is calcium, to prevent eclampsia later on. Both bone-meal and calcium need to be given in conjunction with vitamin D for there to be any benefit. There are proprietary tablets containing both calcium and vitamin D which are quite palatable for the bitch. Vitamin C is not essential in additive form (although some will be gained from fresh fruit and vegetables), as dogs are able to manufacture sufficient for themselves and store it. However, the vet may advise it for anaemia.

Do not give purgatives; a correct diet will avoid constipation. Dog biscuits given whole so that gnawing and crunching goes on will help the situation as will a meal of liver or cod-liver oil capsules. The biscuits will also help to keep the teeth tartar free.

# Exercise

The bitch should rest for a couple of hours after her meal, but it is also important to keep her muscles toned up for whelping. Apart from the exercise, an outing is an excellent way of taking the bitch's mind off herself and she will be far more content to rest quietly on her return. If she can run free so much the better. Let her roam in the garden where she will be keeping her muscles in trim. If exercised in a public park or on a beach, keep her on a flexi-lead as this gives her freedom to run or to wander at her own pace, but you have her under control should a wandering canine friend come up to her. You do not want her to take off into a mad romp at this stage. Once she has had enough, take her home quietly. As she gets heavier she will probably appreciate several short outings in a day rather than one long one. Car journeys should be short and without any swaying around. She should be lifted in and out correctly and not be allowed to jump up and down steps or on and off chairs.

# Lifting a Pregnant Bitch

Bull Terriers, being heavy, should be lifted with an arm round the front of the chest and under the neck, and another behind the back legs, below the tail and above the hocks. Her weight should now be resting on your forearms and all four legs dangling down between your arms. This avoids having to clutch the bitch around the abdomen. Lower her to the floor, and make sure that she is taking her weight on her feet in a well-balanced fashion before releasing her.

# Cleanliness

Bull Terriers are always happy to receive the extra attention that is involved in the daily grooming ritual. A good but gentle brush of the coat gets to the areas such as the back of her neck that are not otherwise easily reached. It is a time that you can check for ear and teeth problems which could cause discomfort when with her pups. It is not advisable to bath a pregnant bitch for risk of a chill; if she needs cleaning prepare a bowl of warm water with a little shampoo added and wash the affected parts with a cloth. I wash their faces and any dirty marks in this manner every day, and they are so used to it that they think nothing of having their ever-increasing under-carriage bathed when whelping time approaches. If for any reason the bitch has to be bathed, or gets really wet as those used to playing in the sea or on a river edge may well do, she should be thoroughly dried (preferably with a hair-dryer), and not allowed to lie about in draughts that may cause her to catch cold.

# Bedding

A bitch's bed needs to be draught-free and soft enough for comfort. The bedding needs to be sufficiently flexible that the bitch can rearrange it according to the requirements of her bulges. A large blanket or carpet forms the basic bedding and then a couple of rugs or blankets of wool or sheepskin provide the comfort.

# Date of Whelping

Canine gestation tables are published in many dog books, diaries and so forth and consist of the date of mating and resultant date when the bitch is due to whelp. This acts as confirmation of your own calculations, bearing in mind the varying number of days in each month. Difficulties in calculation may arise when two matings took place. One of my bitches produced all the pre-whelping signs at the correct time for the first mating to have been successful, but did not produce the pups until sixty-three days after the second mating. Needless to say, the entire household was suffering from nervous exhaustion by the time the vociferous family arrived.

Bull Terriers have been known to present their first whelp sixty-three days to the hour that they were mated. A heavy bitch may have her litter earlier, but whelps born earlier than the fifty-eighth day are often difficult to rear. One of my very healthy, lively litters arrived a week early – the bitch having given warning by bustling up the garden and trying to pick a fight with every Bull Terrier foolish enough to come out into their run as she passed. She was obviously clearing the field for her great event.

If the bitch does not deliver by sixty-five days the vet must be consulted. There can be many reasons for this – the most common being a false pregnancy. This is extremely disappointing. The bitch can go through most of the signs leading up to the whelping itself most convincingly. One bitch went through the whole routine only to go into the garden at the eleventh hour, find her ball and demand a game! Usually, suspicion that all is not as it should be can be roused by looking at the bitch's vulva – could even a tiny whelp get out? If it is not softened and swollen I am very suspicious. Of course with a maiden bitch she may be fooling you and will produce a litter with very few earlier signs. Today it is possible to have the bitch scanned. This will confirm the existence of whelps, though it does not yet guarantee their absence should they be tucked well away. If the bitch has a history of re-absorbing her whelps, this is a very useful service enabling the breeder to know what is going on.

Some owners tell of having taken a lively bitch for a short walk only to be presented with a pup shortly after their return. Every bitch has individual tricks at this time and should you be intending to have more than one litter or have several bitches it is worth recording the details of each bitch and her whelping for reference in the future. Note such details as the day of arrival, early or late; the time between each arrival, minutes or hours; whether veterinary assistance was necessary or not; whether she was good at dealing with the whelps when they first arrived, and so forth.

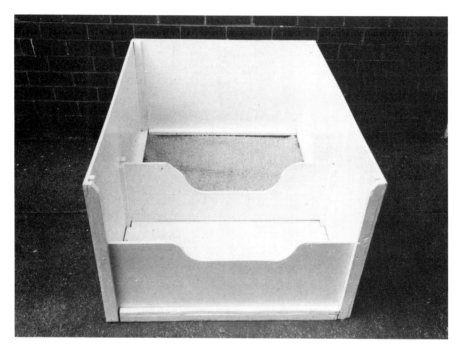

A whelping bed.

# The Whelping Box

The whelping box is the name given to the bed provided for the bitch and her litter. It needs to be of a size to accommodate both. A handyman can make one from new wood that will fit all the requirements but it is possible to adapt an existing wooden box such as a tea-chest or packing case. For several litters I used a four and a half by three foot (1.5 × 1m) wooden drawer lined with a piece of floor vinyl, with a pig rail made from dowling bought locally. Over the years, however, I have adapted ideas and suggestions and I now have the perfect design for my Bull Terrier requirements.

The bed needs to be large enough to enable the bitch to lie on her side, but not so large that the puppies can crawl away from the warmth. It should be raised two or three inches (5–7cm) off the floor to keep out any cold draughts, and the sides and back ought to be two feet (60cm) high to ensure that the bitch is warm and feels secure. Any higher would inhibit the breeder from leaning over to deal with the whelps in the bed. The front has been especially adapted over the years. Originally, I favoured a hinged, drop-down front, but this has been abandoned. A good idea in theory, I found that the hinged gap caught food and hair and presented difficulties for young whelps on their early attempts to brave the world of the kitchen floor. Instead, I have a groove into which the front board can be slotted. It can be completely removed when the whelps want to be adventurous, or when I want to clean the bed and to allow the pregnant mother in and out without needing to jump continually. The centre section of the front board should be cut away and smoothed round. This is so that the bitch can step in and out of the bed when the board is in place without hurting her undercarriage. Her teats will be very large and she will not be accustomed to making allowances for them when negotiating any such barrier. As my bed is four feet (1m) deep I also have grooves at the one foot (30cm) mark so that this front board can be put in place at three feet making a cosier bed for the mother should she obviously prefer it. It also ensures that her whelps cannot crawl too far away. I am able to use the front portion of the bed to kneel on when I wish to attend to the bitch or the litter.

The latest addition is an alternative front board, the same height as the sides. This came about because of a bitch who was restless and nervy, continually leaving her bed to check out the kitchen. I concluded that she did not feel fully secure, and so I made the front board higher, making her feel safe from any intruders. An accidental but very useful feature that I discovered was that our largest dog cage fitted exactly inside the whelping bed and on occasion has been used there. All the wood is painted in a lead-free, high gloss, white paint which is easy to wipe down with disinfectant.

Bull Terrier bitches are notoriously clumsy with their whelps and they will lie down and stretch out quite oblivious to their where-abouts. For this reason it is essential to have an escape area for the whelps. Most whelping boxes therefore have a guard rail or pig rail, so called because of it being used in pig farming for exactly the same reason – to protect the piglets from their mother's weighty body. Having seen a bitch deliberately sit on two whelps to crush them I know how easily it can be done. Pig rails need to be placed around the inside of the bed, approximately three inches (7cm) off the floor. It can be made from an inch (2cm) thick piece of dowling or a length of wood such as a broom handle.

Originally, I fixed one three inches (7cm) away from the sides so that any whelp pushed under the rail by the bitch's body could then

It is a good idea to make the whelping bed large enough to accommodate the dog's cage.

wriggle up and out to safety. However, this only worked in the very early stages as whelps grow so quickly, and they soon became jammed between the pig rail and the side of the bed. I then adopted our present system of detachable lengths of smoothed wood fixed at the ends to fit flush with the sides. They make a ledge about three inches (7cm) from the floor on four sides of the bed. When the bitch leans against this there is room beneath the shelf for the whelp to lie safely. As they grow, I move the ledge higher, giving a five to six inch (12–15cm) safety gap. Eventually, I remove it altogether. Some breeders like to have two loose floors for their whelping boxes so that they are interchangeable, but I find that there are too many nooks and crannies that continually catch hairs and crumbs and constantly need disinfecting.

Pregnant bitches may agree that the whelping box is the place to rear litters, but many consider it to be their bed and do not intend to soil it by whelping there. They will choose some other spot that

The pig rail.

takes their fancy. My bitches tend to favour the isolation unit, maybe because it is safely away from the other Bull Terriers, or possibly because that is where they have received special attention and nursing whenever they have been feeling ill. Other bitches prefer to be where they know I am bound to be – the kitchen! I have now settled for having the whelping bed in the corner of the kitchen – or rather (because of its size), it becomes the main feature of the kitchen, with the breakfast bar and a couple of units being taken out.

I insist that this is where the great event is to be held, though I did have one bitch who had an unexpectedly early litter and presented me with three whelps on the settee. On that occasion we hastily revised our plans and moved the whelping bed into the lounge in time for the remaining four whelps to arrive. We covered the carpet with plastic sheeting which was not a good idea as once wet we were inclined to slip on the plastic and it had to be completely covered with a thick layer of newspaper for safety.

After the puppies have left the whelping bed for good it should be scrubbed out and left to dry in the sun. When brought back into service for the next litter, three or four days in the sunshine will help to kill any loitering germs.

## Whelping Box Bedding

Simulated sheepswool rugs are excellent for bedding. Any wetness goes straight through to the thick wad of newspaper lining the bed, leaving the whelps and mother on a warm dry surface. A useful item is a rubber hot-water bottle, filled with warm but not boiling water and wrapped safely in two covers – one each way – rolled in a towel or piece of woolly blanket with the ends tucked firmly in. Placed in the furthest corner from the bitch's favourite lying position it acts as a surrogate mother for any whelp that has wandered away. It is extremely useful to accustom the whelps to this as it is warm, and wobbles in a similar manner to the bitch's stomach, lulling them into a sense of security. Should the bitch be a wanderer or have to be taken away for any length of time – perhaps to visit the vet – the puppies will not miss her. The hot-water bottle must be checked at each filling to ensure that the bitch has not punctured it with her claws or teeth. Once the whelps are teething it should be removed altogether. If it is the only source of heat then it should be replaced by a wrapped stone bottle. The temperature must be carefully checked as should the way the bottle is wrapped. Exploring whelps are inordinately active when it comes to tunnelling under or through blankets and can easily become trapped.

# Heating

In summer-time or in warm climates, the room temperature should be kept constant at around 60° F (15° C). Combined with the hot-water bottle, this should be sufficient. Special care should be taken during a heat-wave. Keep the premises cool, but do not allow draughts. More often, it is a case of keeping the room warm enough and an infra-red lamp is ideal for this. Hang it above the whelping box with some means of adjusting its height according to the amount of heat required. If the bitch fidgets or starts to pant raise the lamp to reduce the amount of heat. It is surprisingly warm under the lamp as you will discover when dealing with the whelps. It does however ensure that the whelps will be kept warm on the

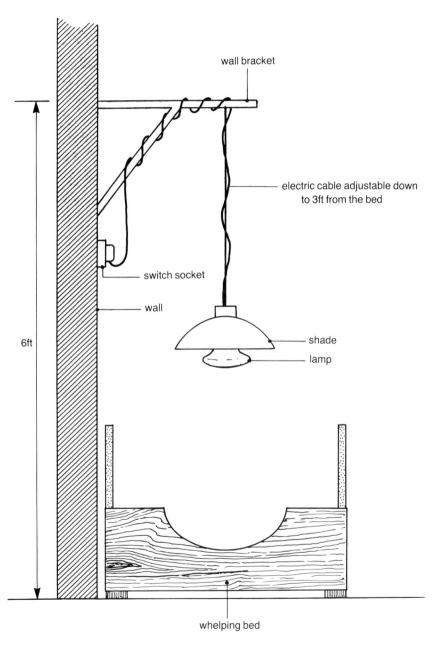

Adjustable heat lamp.

most wintry of nights, even when they have crawled away from the warmth of their mother and brothers and sisters.

# Attendance

Once the whelps have arrived, Bull Terriers have to be watched for the first two weeks. Many breeders set up a camp bed in the whelping room and give constant attendance, others work in two- or three-hour shifts according to how many available helpers are in the household. An over-anxious bitch can turn on her puppies at any time. I have a baby alarm system. There is a microphone suspended from the heat lamp bracket and a small loudspeaker on a very long cable. I can take the loudspeaker into the sitting-room and even with the television set on I can hear the bitch moving around or the whelps crying. One bitch who insisted on going up to the bedroom with her owners rather than staying with her family was quite intrigued by the squawks from the speaker, and lay on the bed with her ears pricked towards the sound. It was not long before she had it worked out, went to sleep and only dashed downstairs when the whelps called for her! She once woke her owners with prods and kisses, and while they dutifully went down and tended to the puppies' needs, she went back to sleep!

On the last few occasions that I have had a litter I have gone a stage further and used a television camera, focused on the whelping bed, with the monitor in the bedroom. This works very well, though care should be taken not to burn the lens with the image of the white bed and white Bull Terriers.

Whereas many breeds prefer to be left alone to have their litters in peace and present you with a beautiful row of clean whelps, Bull Terriers believe in making a great drama of the whole affair. Bull Terrier bitches should not be left unattended during whelping or for the following two weeks. There are many tales of bitches that killed their whelps during the ten minutes in which the owner went off for a cup of coffee. I once saw a bitch kill a whelp that the vet had just returned to the nest after examination. She was not going to allow it back in the bed after being 'contaminated' by the vet. Another bitch is known to have scooped up her pup and run around the room with him, frantic to find what she considered a safe place – the bed evidently was not reaching the required standard. The whelp was punctured in his throat and abdomen by her great canines. The vet had to be called to check the damage, inject the pup to avoid infection and the bitch to calm her down.

If the bitch has built up a good relationship with the breeder she will now be grateful for his or her presence to reassure her that all will be well. I find it very useful to have the whelping bed in the kitchen as it means I can quietly continue with some of the household chores. My bitches do not mind the noise or vibration of the dishwasher and washing-machine, and it is at least one noise that I do not have to familiarise the puppies with when they are older. One bitch was gravely suspicious when I took her dirty bedding to put in the washing-machine – she had to give it a thorough inspection first to make quite sure that I had not taken a puppy as well.

There is no need for the entire household to keep quiet for fear of waking whelps, as they cannot hear yet. However, it is vexing when your bitch has settled down to sleep and the telephone rings or raised voices disturb her. When she rouses, the whelps are woken and the greediest will start the whole family off again in search of another meal.

A bitch who had been particularly affectionate towards me during pregnancy, had a complete change of heart once the whelps arrived. She would dash out of the bed trampling over her whelps without any regard for their safety in order to prevent me moving about. She stopped short of touching me and would dash back to the whelps. For their sake we had a role swop and I took charge of the rest of the kennels while someone else danced attendance on the bitch. Another breeder confirmed this behaviour when he described his bitch as being determined to have his feet off if he dared to move. As he was wont to doze off in a chair and shuffle his feet in his sleep, he decided to go away and leave her to fend for herself. She turned out to be an excellent mother rearing her pups without assistance. Yet another bitch was helped through her whelping and having the bed tidied up, when she decided she would not tolerate the assistant in the room any more. When I arrived home and was told of the situation, I walked purposefully into the room and across to the opposite end from the whelping box. I casually greeted the bitch without even looking at her. She came out to greet me, and made an increasing fuss as she realised that I was not going to take any notice of her, until she positively asked me to go and see what she had produced in her bed. There was no more nonsense after that.

I give you these examples of some bitches' behaviour after whelping to illustrate the variation from one bitch to another. More serious cases will need veterinary assistance, for instance where eclampsia or peritonitis is suspected, but others can benefit from an aspirin given with their warm milk and glucose, before settling down to rest after the final whelp has arrived. The best situations are when the bitch is content, knowing instinctively just what to do and when. The assistant's role is then merely to keep the food supplied, the bed clean and dry, the bitch clean and the whelps from straying too far.

# 11

# Whelping

## Preparation

In order to get the pregnant bitch used to the idea of the whelping bed being her residence for the next couple of months, it is advisable to put her into it at least two weeks before whelping is due. I sink the bitch's own bed into the whelping box for a day or two so that she feels at home and then remove the interior bed leaving her with extra room for her ever increasing bulk. A week or so before the date of whelping a collection should be made of all the items that may be required, so that everything is to hand should events start prematurely. These should include the following:

**Cardboard Box**  This ought to be of a suitable size for the wrapped and protected hot-water bottle to fit snuggly in the bottom, leaving no gaps in which small helpless whelps can become wedged, and with a layer of warm material such as a piece of fleecy flannelette sheeting, covering the bottle to make a warm bed for the whelps should you require it. If the bitch has difficulties in delivering her later whelps and needs to visit the surgery, then the whelps already born will need to be kept warm until her return. Some breeders remove the whelps when the next one is imminent in order to prevent them getting trampled as the bitch turns around or scratches the bedding, or from being soaked when the next whelp arrives. It is far safer to have them tucked away in a box, which can be left in a corner of the bed so that the bitch knows where they are and can nuzzle them, but some bitches get very worked up if the whelps are removed and try lifting them out of their snug box to bury them elsewhere. If this is the case, it is as well to tuck them under the pig rail as soon as the bitch's attention is diverted to the newest arrival. Bull Terriers really do seem to be unaware of where they put their feet. When a seasoned brood bitch was brought in to have her third and last litter, she bustled around inspecting the arrangements, but would not settle down – something was not in order. Eventually she spotted the cardboard box which had been left in the utility room until nearer the event. She vociferously demanded it, and when put on the floor, she carried it to the whelping bed! It then was poked and prodded with her nose until I put the water bottle and blankets in. Her last whelping had been a caesarian section and I rather think she expected all whelps to turn up neatly presented in cardboard boxes.

**Newspaper** A collection of newspaper is one of the requirements when preparing for a litter. Neighbours and friends can be called upon to make a collection of clean newspaper, though we are careful only to accept it from households that do not themselves possess a dog. This is a time when one becomes super sensitive to the possibility of germs and disease being transmitted from other dogs. Newspaper is used in vast quantities during whelping – to line the whelping box and the surrounding floor, for the bitch to tear at when whelping and later on for the puppies to use until they learn to go outside. Some old but clean pieces of blanket or material should also be collected during the weeks of pregnancy.

**Plastic Bags** A supply of plastic bin liners, sacks or paper sacks saved from the delivery of dog meal and biscuits, will be necessary to take the soiled newspaper.

**Bathing Equipment** A couple of flannels and towels – one for the face and one for the rear parts – should be available for the bitch.

### Medical and Other Supplies
Cotton wool balls.
Antiseptic.
Liquid paraffin.
Paper tissues or kitchen roll.
A pair of round-ended scissors boiled for three minutes and left in the cooled water, or steeped in a small dish of alchohol.
Small, warmed towel for drying whelps.
Weighing machine.
Paper and biro to record the time of birth and description, including sex, of each whelp. A note of any markings such as a dark right ear is useful for identification.
Brandy in case it is needed – by bitch or breeder!

# Signs of Whelping

Three days before the bitch is due to whelp it is a wise precaution, particularly if she is a maiden bitch, to visit the vet to check that all is well and that he is aware of the imminent litter. Should he then be called to the whelping he will have an idea of what to expect. In the case of an experienced brood bitch, I phone the surgery to warn them of the approaching event, so that whoever is on duty is aware that he may be called out.

Although behaviour varies between bitches there are some general tendencies. One of the earliest signs of pregnancy is the bitch refusing her food and her temperature dropping from 101°F to around 98°F (39°C to around 37°C.) If it is a bitch's first litter she may appear apprehensive and restless and whimper or cry. However, some brood bitches do not show any anxiety, and appear to be very rested. Two days before one bitch was due to whelp I departed for a show, confident that she had no intention of presenting me with her litter that day. She appeared to be glad to see me go so that she could get on with her sleep. When I phoned home at lunch-time the kennel manager informed me that there were already three healthy whelps, and the vet was still on the premises.

Some bitches are very active, tearing their blankets, scratching in corners feverishly and rearranging their bedding. One bitch sat in her box ripping up a pair of jeans as if they were made of tissue paper. Another tore a strong cardboard box to shreds with violent jerks of her head. It is very useful to have adequate supplies of such tough but destructable items on hand, should your bitch prove to be one of the restless ones. A favourite exercise of three of my bitches is to dash out into the garden and have a frantic dig in one particular flower-bed, rushing back to the whelping bed to deposit soil and peat from their feet on the clean bedding! It has become such a ritual that we now remove the plants and leave the flower-bed for the bitches!

A maiden bitch will not show any signs of milk until labour actually starts, but an experienced bitch will have milk three or four days beforehand. An older bitch will have a 'sunken' appearance once the puppies have dropped, but this is not obvious in a maiden bitch whose muscles will be far tighter. Most bitches will lie in the typical Bull Terrier pose – on their stomach with legs stretched out fore and aft. It always seems to me to be so uncomfortable. It is almost as if they are trying to push the puppies out!

155

During the last few days, the vulva will soften and swell and at about the time of the temperature drop and the onset of labour, a thick sticky mucus is discharged. It may be most noticeable as the bitch returns from relieving herself outside. It is important to keep the bitch clean after a trip outside – wash her undercarriage and anywhere that is soiled gently, then grease her tail and hocks with vaseline as this will aid cleaning after the event is completed. A soft, close-fitting house collar of nylon or leather should be worn during whelping. From anything between one hour and twenty-four hours the bitch may have fits of trembling which can be a good indication that events are on the way. At the first sign of straining a note should be made of the time and of the interim period between each effort. She will usually press her rear against the sides of the bed and push hard. Some bitches prefer to whelp standing up. Eventually the contractions can be seen and felt, the bitch relaxing and panting between each. Panting can often be the first visible sign that labour has started. It takes about one and a half hours for a maiden bitch to present her first puppy.

# Birth of the Whelps

Each whelp is surrounded by a membrane which contains placenta and the umbilical cord through which the whelp receives oxygen and nourishment. The whelp is protected on all sides by amniotic fluid which acts as a shock absorber and cushion. During the birth contractions, the membrane sac is pushed forward through the birth canal, enlarging it and washing it out for the whelp when it bursts. The whelp will still be in an inner bag, the membrane of which is broken by the bitch to enable the whelp to breath.

The appearance of the 'water-bag' should not be mistaken for the whelp. It is a sac of greenish black fluid that surrounds and cushions the whelp. Its size and shape vary, depending on how long the journey has taken. It can resemble a string of dark beads if labour has been prolonged. The bag often appears and then disappears before finally bursting from pressure or from being licked by the bitch. You can tell the difference between the water-bag and the whelp by gently feeling the swelling above the vulva – if it is hard and solid it is the whelp's head, if it is soft, it will be the water-bag. The whelp should follow shortly after the water-bag, head first with forefeet tucked under the neck. It will be expelled in one effort.

The bitch may sit for a few minutes after this and not seem to notice her whelp. She may immediately start eating the placenta rather than attending to the whelp. Do not panic! The whelp is still attached to and gathering last drops of nutrient from the placenta by the umbilical cord. This placenta or 'after-birth' looks like a mass of raw liver. The bitch should break the membrane to allow the whelp to breathe, sever the cord and eat the placenta. Bull Terriers are often too shocked to carry out these tasks immediately, but the good mothers in the breed soon get themselves organised. You should gently remove the membrane covering the whelp's head and mouth to enable it to breath, and then hold it out to the bitch to lick. The bitch should sever the cord; however, under- or overshot jaws make this more difficult and the bitches are inclined to pull the cord with their teeth while trying to sever it. This can drag the whelp and cause a hernia. If the bitch is not making an efficient attempt, sever the cord yourself.

If possible, and if the whelp is breathing well, leave it attached to the cord for a few minutes. Stroke the blood in the cord towards the whelp, giving it the benefit of the extra nourishment. To sever it, pinch the cord between finger and thumb about an inch (2½cm) from the puppy and with the other hand half an inch (1cm) further on. Disjoin it by pulling the hand nearest the whelp towards it or cut with sterile scissors. Squeezing the end of the cord tightly should eventually stop any haemorrhage, but should it not stop bleeding, a ligature on the cord end made with silk thread may be necessary.

Placenta is rich in iron and protein which are very nourishing for the bitch, but too much can give her loose, black motions and if possible I usually whip one or two of the placentas away. If she makes a fuss about it I leave well alone as she has plenty to get neurotic about without my adding to it. As a result of eating the placentas she will not require solid food for the first couple of days. The placenta and membranes usually come away with the whelp, but they may be delayed until the next contraction. It is very important to observe that the placenta has been expelled. Occasionally it does not come away until the arrival of the next whelp but should it be left behind after the last whelp the vet must be called and an injection given to bring it away before it turns putrid.

The bitch should lick the whelp to stimulate the heart and lungs. She will roll it around the bed before pushing it towards the teats and settling down with it. Some Bull Terriers are far too excited at this stage and may be excessively rough, rolling the whelp against

157

the sides of the bed. The breeder should then take over and try to stimulate the whelp by gently rubbing it dry in a warmed towel. Once the bitch settles down with her whelp offer her a drink of warm milk with glucose, letting her rest before the whole procedure starts again. A puppy an hour is about the Bull Terrier average, and if she starts to strain but does not produce anything in an hour, the vet should be called.

Some Bull Terriers are excellent mothers and can safely be left to get on with the task in hand. Depending upon the number of whelps and the disposition of the bitch, I often slot the front board of the whelping bed into the grooves, foreshortening the bed but still leaving plenty of room for the mother to lie on her side and for the whelps with their hot-water bottle. This relieves some mothers of anxiety when a whelp sets off in the wrong direction. It is very difficult for her to get a whelp back when the rest of the litter are snugly feeding from her. Often the bitch will growl and although the whelp cannot hear, it can sense the vibrations and will turn for home. The bitch may appear to be preventing one particular pup

A proud mother with ten-day-old puppies.

from coming to the milk but there is usually a very good reason for this. She is probably well aware that this greedy fellow has been clambering over all the other whelps, helping himself to the best supplied teats and generally pushing everyone else aside. The assistant should keep a careful watch on any such behaviour on the part of the bitch, and check that the isolated whelp has had a meal.

A bitch may dislike a particular whelp, and there is nearly always justifiable cause. If there is some deformity, such as a cleft palate, the bitch may push the whelp away, rolling it aside from warmth and nourishment. However, some bitches are so overwrought that a whelp will not suck, that they will constantly lick and stimulate it, ignoring the healthy members of the family. Patient observation will enable you to recognise these situations. Only very occasionally will the family be too large for the bitch to cope, but if this should be the case, it will be helpful to divide the litter, putting one half in the cage (within the whelping bed), and leaving the rest with the bitch in the remaining section of the bed.

A timer or an alarm clock is essential to remind you of 'change over' times – every two hours, gradually lengthening as the feeds become further apart. After a while the whelps will become so used to this arrangement that they will wake automatically when it is their time to feed. Some bitches are best taken away from their whelps and brought back at feeding and cleaning time. Providing the first bond has been made between bitch and whelps the bitches seem to accept separation quite readily.

# Complications

There are some complications which arise quite frequently but can be overcome with a little positive intervention. The assistant should not be afraid to help but should not be interfering continually when help is not required, as this only agitates the bitch.

## Large Whelp

Older bitches are more likely to have varying sized whelps with one or two being much larger than the others. The lowest whelp arrives first and is often the largest and most difficult. If the bitch is having problems pushing the whelp out, you will need to assist. Wash your hands thoroughly, and put some vaseline or cream on one of your

159

fingers. Insert the finger and hook it around the whelp, if possible over the back of its neck. When the bitch strains, pull the whelp steadily down and outwards. If the difficulty persists call the vet. If the head is visible but the shoulders or body are stuck, break the membrane around the mouth to allow it to breathe, then grasp below the head between two fingers and gently pull down and towards the bitch. Once a little more is protruding the whelp can be held in a small piece of towelling or a wad of cotton wool. When the bitch strains whelps can be gently and steadily eased downwards and towards the bitch's abdomen. If the bitch appears exhausted give her two to three teaspoonfuls of brandy in her milk.

## Breech Presentation

This is where the whelp emerges the wrong way round – the hind feet and tail arriving first. If the membrane has broken, the whelp will suffocate or become entangled in the placenta. It is also dangerous for the bitch in that the next whelp may have started on its way and will become entangled with the breech. All her efforts to expel these whelps will be exhausting the bitch, and you must intervene.

Hold the protruding legs gently but firmly in a wad of cotton wool to prevent them disappearing again. A steady pull without clenching the legs too firmly (which could lame the whelp), even when the bitch is not straining, should release the whelp. If the shoulders are wedged, gently pull to one side to release one shoulder and then to the other. If it is having difficulty coming away, stand the bitch, place your left hand under her abdomen and raise it gently. Watch carefully for the placenta to arrive as otherwise it may cause problems for the next whelp, or be left behind and cause complications for the bitch.

## Caesarean Section

If there are difficulties due to a large whelp or the bitch becoming exhausted from some unknown cause, you must call the vet. It may be necessary to remove the whelps by an operation.

Modern anaesthetics allow the bitch to regain consciousness relatively quickly after the operation but the whelps (which are often stronger than those born normally), should be put in their prepared cardboard box so that the bitch has a chance to become completely conscious. She should then be handed one pup at a time to lick and suckle. A careful watch should be kept to ensure she accepts her puppies. If it is a large litter, supplementary feeding for a few days will help the bitch to regain her strength.

## Calcium Deficiency

Calcium deficiency usually appears in the bitch within days of whelping, sometimes three hours in a Bull Terrier. The signs and the treatment are similar to those for eclampsia.

## Eclampsia

Eclampsia is sometimes known as milk fever and can occur at three to four weeks after whelping, when the puppies are being weaned. The first signs are that the bitch pants excessively, becomes agitated, lifts her puppies and carries them around, and has glazed eyes. Her temperature will be lower than normal, she may froth at the mouth and in the latter stages, may have convulsions. She must have help at once. The vet will give her a calcium injection which will make her calm down in a short while. If the vet is not immediately available, a sandwich containing several Calcidee tablets can help if given early enough. Make a note of the dosage so that you can inform your vet when he arrives and he may adjust his dosage accordingly.

## After-Care

When whelping is finished, rest and sleep are the best restoratives. Small quantities of egg and milk or baby cereals should be given at first, working up to light meals, milky puddings, poached fish, chicken and finally to her ordinary diet. Once all the pups have arrived and the bitch has settled down to rest, inform the vet of the results and ask him to visit to examine the bitch, and to give her an injection of calcium or pituitary as necessary. He can then check the pups for any abnormality.

The whelps may stop sucking if the milk has not come down. In this case cover the teats in a thick glucose and water mixture and then put the puppies to them. Their sucking is essential to stimulate the milk glands. The whelps can seem very obstinate and they may clamp their jaws together, so determined patience is necessary to

161

persuade them to work at the teats. Do not give in – it may be the difference between life and death for the puppies. Mix up some dried puppy milk, sweeten it with glucose, mix and feed to the whelps from a baby's feeding bottle every two hours. If her milk has not come down in forty-eight hours call the vet.

## Mastitis

Mastitis can be caused by inflammation of the mammary glands, where whelps have favoured one or two particular teats and ignored others. Assistants noting this should move whelps on to the other glands periodically. The bitch will be restless, off her food and be running a high temperature. The affected glands will be swollen and have hard lumps. They will be hot, inflamed and very tender. Bathe with hot water every half hour to soften the gland, and lubricate the teat gently to expel some of the milk. Once it has started to flow, a hungry pup will do the rest providing the bitch is willing. Usually, bitches will put up with a great deal of discomfort if it involves feeding their puppies. This state however should not have arisen, and would not have done if the teats had been cared for by the assistant after each feed. If there is only one whelp, persuade it to sample all the teats in turn. With less demand the milk supply will usually diminish naturally. Should there be signs of an abscess forming veterinary advice must be taken. Antibiotics will clear this up quite quickly.

## Metritis

Metritis is inflammation of the uterus due to infection either from poor conditions or from such causes as an unborn whelp being left behind. There will be a rise in temperature, discharge and gasped breaths. If not treated the bitch will die. Keep her warm and dry and call your veterinary surgeon immediately. Antibiotics given after the whelping usually prevent this condition.

## Umbilical Hernia

This is caused by either the bitch or the handler tugging on the whelp's abdomen as the umbilical cord is severed. A very small hernia will disappear naturally but in more severe cases will develop into an ugly lump like a button. A vet will check this for you when giving the pups their after birth examination. It is possible to bind up their tummies using a small piece of cotton wool on the hernia and a tiny slice from a cork over the cotton wool, all bound round with one inch (2½cm) wide adhesive tape. This should be applied diagonally to form a cross over it and then once straight round. Then cover with a bandage and stitch into place as the bitch will probably lick and fuss at the tape. The whelp can be kept in a warm box, hand-held to the teat to be fed and held out to the bitch for cleaning afterwards.

# 12

# Rearing

## Feeding

At two and a half weeks old puppies can be tempted to lap. This is easier if the meal is of a creamy consistency. A little Farley's Baby Cereal or Farex, with a touch of glucose and mixed with warm milk to a semi-fluid state offered on a saucer or shallow dish is the best for the pup to experiment. Most puppies get the idea quite quickly. It should be offered immediately before they have a meal from mum so that they are hungry enough to want to try to lap, sufficiently awake to be interested and old enough to be wanting to experiment with all they come across.

We use the opportunity of feeding to start the pups on their socialisation programme. They will have already become accustomed to being handled. When being picked up out of the nursery bed for any reason, I warn them first by stroking the nape of their neck and down their back. Remember they cannot hear or see that you are around. After being weighed or for whatever reason they were disturbed, they are then put back in a warm place preferably snuggled up to their mother or brothers and sisters, making sure that they are securely supported before releasing them. They must not be allowed to drop the last few inches from your hand, or roll down the side of the hot-water bottle.

Several pieces of terry towelling or similar are very useful at feeding time. I sit down with a piece of towelling across my knees and a puppy resting on my lap, securely held by one hand and slowly introduce him to semi-liquid food. A finger dipped in the mix is offered to the puppy who will grasp it as he would a teat, and then suck. After a few mouthfuls, gradually lower your finger towards the saucer until the pup tries to help himself by lapping at the food. This may take two or three feeds to achieve, but they usually get the idea pretty swiftly.

Occasionally they obstinately refuse to contemplate such food, knowing full well that mum will eventually turn up. In this case I move on to egg custards which are very popular. The bitch usually fusses around when the pups are first being introduced to food, so give her a little on your finger and also let her clean your hand which is probably covered in the stuff by now! Let her lick a little from the same saucer if necessary and she will usually put her seal of approval on it all, sit down and watch, knowing that she will be having most of it eventually when she clears it off the whelp's face, head, paws, tummy and wherever else it has managed to spread. I have seen a bitch lick the mixture off the saucer, put her tongue in the puppy's mouth and tip the mixture in, and then lick his face until the food was swallowed. She then repeated the procedure. After a few turns like this mother kept her nose in the dish while the pup decided to try for himself. It is scenes like this that make puppy rearing so fascinating, lifting it well beyond the realms of profit and loss.

When a puppy appears to be getting less than his tough brothers and sisters it is possible to leave a supply of the milk-food on a saucer under the pig rail for him to have extra. This is referred to as creep feeding. I have not found it very successful as far as the weaklings are concerned. The toughest little fellow is sure to find it first and add to his diet, or else the bitch clears it up when tidying her domain.

The puppies must be introduced only to one new food at a time, so once you have established what it is that they will take, keep to it until they have got used to it and their digestive tracts can cope. At this age always finish with a drink from the bitch or milk from the bottle if that is what they are accustomed to. It settles their stomachs and the bitch feels that she is still in charge of her family's welfare. They are going to need her for some time and her mammary glands need the stimulation. The bitch then will clean up the puppies and make sure that they have relieved themselves – she will go on licking at the pup until he does so. If there is only one puppy, she may wash him to excess and he will become chapped and sore through being continually wet. If being hand-reared this stimulating job must be done by the assistant using a damp piece of cotton wool.

At three weeks the puppies should be introduced to raw meat. This must be free of any fat or gristle, slightly warm (never feed puppies chilled meat) and pounded to a pulp. Teaspoonfuls of meat can then be rolled between the fingers into tiny balls and offered to

Puppies will want to remain close to their mother for some time.

the puppy one at a time. Puppies do not need persuading to eat raw meat, and they will vacuum the whole lot up in one scoop if given the chance. An alternative method is to nail a lump of raw, lean beef to a wooden board and let the puppies suck at it. Bull Terriers enjoy this but need watching as their strong jaws are capable of pulling off a lump, which could choke them.

Weaning progresses slowly, until by four weeks old, the pup should be taking three, hourly feeds of egg custard or Farley's or raw meat or milk from mother. An extra offer of food before their milk top-up as late as possible before you go to bed will assist in keeping the puppies quiet until a civilised hour in the morning

'What shall we do next?'

when the bitch can give them a morning feed. If she is still sleeping with them at this stage they will no doubt have helped themselves during the night! This is where the baby alarm system comes into its own as you can have the speaker in your bedroom and monitor what is going on without the bitch being troubled by your interference.

The meat ration should increase gradually at a ratio of one ounce (25g) of meat a day per week of life – that is half an ounce (12g) per meal. It should be given at the same points in the daily timetable. They should not be given too much at first or they will not be hungry for milk which is essential to prevent them from becoming dehydrated. This increase is a stable guide right through puppyhood until they are having a pound of meat a day. The other meals should become more solid too, including baby rusks, rice puddings and cereals and eventually, at six weeks, ground wholemeal dog meal and biscuit which should be stirred into the meat and moistened with warm bone stock. By five to six weeks puppies should be receiving four milk meals and two meat meals per day.

As the puppies grow, some develop a preference for less sweet foods. Scrambled eggs can be very useful here. The microwave oven has made puppy feeding so much easier than in the past. An egg custard is ready in moments instead of having to be planned in advance. Care should be taken however to allow any puppy food that has been heated in the microwave to cool down.

The bitch will clean up after the puppies in the early stages, but once they are starting to eat other foods she will become less willing, and when they are wormed, that is usually the signal for her to cease altogether. If the whelping bed is small, or has the half-way barrier in place, the confined area will encourage the pups to climb out of the bed to relieve themselves. If the area is large they will be inclined to crawl over to a vacant area in the bed, which is an unfortunate habit to cure later on in their lives. I have had this problem arise twice, on both occasions when only one whelp survived in the litter.

# Worming

All puppies should be treated for worms. There are several preparations on the market, but I prefer to acquire worming tablets from my veterinary surgeon. There is an injection that can be given to older puppies, for dogs need to be be wormed regularly throughout their lives. They can be carrying several types of worm, but roundworm and tapeworm are the most common, with heartworm prevalent in the more tropical areas. All puppies have roundworms. These look like flexible strings pointed at both ends, and they usually coil up or loop over when first emitted. Infested puppies can pass them in their stools, or throw them up in a coughing bout but the most common evidence is a distended, hard stomach after a meal. The worms damage the puppies' tissues and in severe cases block and even perforate the intestines. The puppy will become out of condition with a dry coat and dandruffy skin, and can become seriously depleted of vitamin B, which is absorbed by the worms.

Worming should be carried out when the puppies are four weeks old to prevent the worm larvae migrating around their bodies which happens between five and six weeks of age. The correct dosage must be adhered to and some precaution taken to ensure that no puppy accidentally receives a second dose. I take each puppy in turn, popping the pills down their throats and returning them to the whelping bed. That way I try to avoid getting confused as to who has had their treatment and who has not. The pup's mouth should be opened and the required dose placed on the back of the throat. Push it in with a finger, shut the mouth and stroke the throat until it has been swallowed down. The puppy should be watched carefully to ensure that he has not pushed the tablet to the side of his mouth to spit it out later or that he does not vomit the tablet up again. The first round of tablets usually goes down without too much trouble as it is a new experience. It is on later occasions that the tricks will be tried!

# Care of the Bitch

Throughout nursing, care should be taken with the bitch's under-carriage. It should be washed carefully on returning from an out-door excursion so that the teats are clean for the pups to feed. A lanolin cream should be applied after a feed, particularly once the pups have needle-sharp little teeth appearing through their gums. The whole of the area will need some cool, soothing lotion if the pups have been scratching with their claws. Any evidence of this should be followed up by using an emery board on the culprit's nails. It is important too to check down the fold between the two rows of teats. It becomes very sweaty, particularly if the teats are pendulous, and needs washing and carefully drying off, otherwise it can become sore. Great care should be taken as to what cream is used on the whole area, as any harmful ingredients could be assimilated through the skin and into the milk.

Gradually the bitch will leave her pups for longer periods and not sit for so long at any one time to let them feed. They will, of course, run to her whenever she passes by, but they will soon give up when they find there is no milk. She should be encouraged to leave her pups. Lead her away to her favourite sunny spot in the house, or put her back in her kennel for a couple of hours. She will appreciate a good sleep and be suprisingly content. I have the puppy play-pen erected in the lounge or the garden and with the pups safely inside, the bitch can rest unmolested while they play, but she is still ready to answer their cries for help. One bitch, who had taken herself off to the bedroom for a bit of peace and quiet came dashing downstairs when a puppy was choking. He had nipped a leaf off a house-plant which had then stuck across the back of his throat. When mother arrived, I had prised the pup's mouth open but could not move the damp leaf which was clinging there. The bitch whipped her tongue into the pup's mouth and brought out the leaf.

Eventually, the bitch should be given drier meals, with reduced amounts of milk to help dry up her milk supply. She should be given supplements continuing with the calcium and vitamin D for a few weeks. Should she be out of coat (which may be the result of being under a heat-lamp), a course of vitamin A will help her to recover the hair. A little corn oil or a small lump of margerine on her main meal will condition the coat. Some bitches acquire bare patches, particularly down the sides of their abdomens, which can be evidence of a hormone imbalance. This should rectify itself once she is restored to full fitness again. If not, she may need a hormone injection from the vet.

# Mealtime Routine

Young puppies should have become used to being stroked and fondled in the whelping bed and later in the assistant's arms while being fed. Now is the time when all the family can be called upon to help. Everyone in the house should have a puppy on their lap at feeding time. The pups become used to being passed from one to another and being moved to another position or having the food dish removed for a few moments while the handler deals with some emergency. I have never had to cure an older pup or an adult dog from growling at anyone interfering with him or his meal and I put this down to constant handling at mealtime at an early age. It is an occasion when the family have the opportunity to feel they are being useful and can get to know the puppies, though you should remember to emphasise the need for scrupulous cleanliness. An eighty-year-old aunt of ours always enjoys this stage, once the puppies are three to four weeks old and she can hold them on her lap and encourage them to eat. It is interesting to see the bond she builds up with them and her interest in them develop as each pup progresses to adulthood.

At between four and five weeks of age, the pups are ready to help themselves to their food. They should be provided with a dish of food each and watched. The greediest, having devoured his own, will try to push his slower neighbour off his food dish. Once the edge is off their appetite you may find the entire litter moving around and investigating what has been left by the others. A careful note should be made of which puppies have not eaten sufficiently and these can be individually fed later. The greedy ones should be discouraged from stuffing themselves at the expense of their brothers and sisters but at the same time this interchanging in an amicable manner is good training for the future. They do not develop obsessive tendencies at mealtime. On no account should the puppies be fed from one large dish – how can you possibly tell if each pup has had sufficient for his needs? The greediest will have been behaving like a suction pump while another, who is experimenting with a newly cut tooth, will have not taken in a quarter of his bodily requirements.

Always have a supply of clean water available. Check that the water-bowl is truly clean, not just topped up with fresh water. A slimy deposit, which can be felt by running your fingers across the bowl, clings to the dish and can only be removed by a thorough wash.

A diet sheet should be drawn up of exactly what each puppy likes and dislikes and what quantity of each foodstuff to give and when. Thus, when he leaves home the diet sheet goes with him and he can be kept on the same food and near to the same routine until he has settled into his new surroundings.

# Care of Teeth

The milk teeth come through as sharp pin-points and need to grow straight. Chewable toys such as a nylon bone should be provided to help with the growth. A marrow bone makes an excellent toy as well as providing nourishment if the pups can get the marrow out. Watch that mother does not remove it as being unsuitable for her babies, but just right for her! Sterilised bones from the pet shop make very adequate substitutes.

# Ears

At about ten days onwards the ears of the young puppy start to unfold. Some start to come up while the pups are still with the bitch. Each puppy must be checked for deafness. The kindest course of action if the puppy is deaf is to have it put down. A dog has a hazardous life ahead of him if he cannot hear. Bull Terrier Club members agree when joining the Club not to breed from deaf Bull Terriers. The result of this policy has considerably diminished hereditary deafness, though it still comes through occasionally. Pups should be able to hear by six weeks but there may be some late developers. If a puppy is still deaf by eight weeks it is considered extremely unlikely that he will ever hear.

Testing with a loud noise behind an unsuspecting pup is one method of identifying deafness – a bell ringing, a squeaky toy or clapping hands. One puppy here did not respond to any noise, but we made excuses for her. Being the only one in the litter she was inclined to please herself about what she did and when. Without the noise of brothers and sisters she did not need to react to their calls. However, when she reached six weeks I tested her seriously and found that she completely ignored everything we did. Sadly, I agreed that a trip to the vet was indicated. The following morning a low flying plane passed overhead, shaking the house. The pup and I were in the garden and the ground shook beneath our feet. She jumped and reacted as if she had heard the noise and was frightened. I told myself that she was reacting to vibrations only, but from that moment on she could quite clearly hear. Her ears had at last opened and now the rustle of a biscuit packet can be heard from the furthest corner of the house.

# Eyes

The eyes open from ten days onwards and may need a little damp cotton wool to remove any stickiness, or even some eye ointment. At first there is a mere glint and then a slit opening appears. Their eyes will need protection from daylight for the first week or so and they are unable to focus their eyes for several days. When they can see, they start their explorations in earnest!

# Integration

Once the puppies are ready to explore, the front is removed from the whelping bed and they can step in and out without having to clamber over the barrier. Then the world is open to them. Adventuring forth and then running for the safety of the bed occupies their waking hours for a few days. Then the more daring of them will start looking for mischief. Electrical equipment must be checked to ensure wires and cables are tucked out of reach.

One breeder tells how she returned to the kitchen to discover that an entire litter had vanished. In disbelief she searched the kitchen cupboards and fitments, then the entire downstairs floor of the house. There was no sight of five healthy puppies. Had someone entered through the back door and stolen them? If so, why did the bitch not raise the alarm? Had they somehow got into the rest of the house? The bitch continued her contented dozing in the bed. Nearly frantic, the breeder dragged the bitch out of the bed and told her to find them. With an obvious sigh, the bitch shook herself and then swaggered over to some corner units and pushed. The facia board in the corner was loose at the bottom and behind it were all five pups curled up fast asleep. The bitch strolled back to her bed leaving the pups in their new resting place!

When it is time to settle the pups down in the whelping bed for their rest, the barrier is put back. Once they try to climb this we place a cushion on the outside for them to land on. At night, the alternative high front board is used to keep them in their bed. Each evening these youngsters are nursed by anyone sitting in the lounge. They are caressed, have their tummies tickled, their teeth looked at and are put down to run on the carpet and picked up again. All this is usually to the accompaniment of the piano, the radio, the television or people's voices.

Exploring the world is fun but full of potential danger. Curtains to swing on, table-cloth corners to pull, slippery floor surfaces to slither upon – all need to be investigated. The use of a puppy play-pen does give the handler some freedom and once enclosed the bitch will often keep a quiet eye on the scene from a safe distance, raising the alarm if necessary. However, one of my bitches insisted on being allowed in with her pups. If we did not put her in the play-pen then she would jump and scramble over the top, wrecking everything! It is possible to convert a child's play-pen which can be purchased second-hand. One with a floor keeps the lounge carpet clean and free from wet patches. The lower portion of the sides can be surrounded with some material while the whelps are small enough to wriggle through the bars and particularly when they are of the size for getting jammed between them. There are excellent folding metal play-pens specially designed for puppies on the market. For outdoor use, I particularly favour one to which extra side pannels can be added to make the play-pen larger when the puppies require more space. This type also has the advantage that two of the side panels can be clipped to a folding cage providing a bed area for whenever the pups wish to retire. This play-pen is without a floor and it gives the pups a chance to discover grass! It should be checked fairly often to ensure that there is still a shady section if the sun is hot and that it is protected from draughts.

Puppies should not be allowed to get bored. A selection of their toys should be placed in the play-pen and then changed over after the novelty has worn off. Take care not to leave them with breakable plastic, sticks or small objects that could be swallowed. A cardboard box in the centre of the play-pen is full of potential – it can be run around, jumped in and on and dragged along with pride!

At around six weeks I put the cage into the whelping bed with the puppies' blankets, hot-water bottle and toys. The heat lamp is raised to reduce the temperature, unless it is mid-winter. After a few nights in their new bed I then remove the whelping bed for scrubbing out and storing until the next time. The cage is left in exactly the same place with plenty of newspaper in front. All that has gone is their surrounding barrier. Once they have grown used to this, I produce a well-lined cardboard box and blankets and a plastic dog bed similarly fitted out. These are left adjacent to the cage. The pups then have three beds to choose from and after playing in and out of each, they will settle down to sleep – often all in one bed – but at least they have met the different types of bed and will not be frightened when they encounter a new one in strange surroundings.

Puppy play can become quite rough and you will probably hear some growling. Tug of war games with an old slipper or piece of blanket will become familiar sights. Occasionally there will be a serious fight, particularly between boys who, by sixteen weeks, will be fighting for dominance. They are capable of tearing ears or marking each other for life. The only time when two of my puppies had a set-to, their mother barged in between them and while I whisked one away she took on the other. She picked him up by the scruff of his neck and shook him – hard!

I have had the fascinating experience of watching a bitch teach her puppies how to fight. She was a most gentle Bull Terrier and I was amazed that she knew how to fight, let alone how to provide a step by step instruction course to her offspring. First, she would pick one puppy from the rest of the litter and take him a little distance away. Then she would stand with her chest like a brick wall while the puppy had to try to use his weight to knock her off balance. After a few minutes of this the bitch gave him a good wash and sent him back to the litter. She then collected another pup from the group and started all over again. A few days later I discovered that the pups had advanced to a second stage where they were to go for their opponent's throat. This meant that the bitch was losing lumps of hair from around her neck and cheeks and at this stage, I decided that the training had gone far enough.

# Departure Time

When the puppies reach six to eight weeks of age, you must decide which puppies you want to keep and which are to go to new homes. Although they should be weaned and capable of leaving home at six weeks it is preferable to keep them for eight, as not only are their

Time to say goodbye.

stomachs stronger by then but the bitch is less perturbed by their leaving. At six weeks she will search the premises for them, but at eight, she will come out to the car and positively wave them goodbye! On returning to the house she will probably go and play with her ball or do some other activity which she enjoys and which strictly does not include puppies. In the wild, she would have rejoined the pack by this time.

With the puppy should go the copy of his pedigree and the registration papers (subject to their receipt from the Kennel Club), the transfer on the reverse duly filled out. A diet sheet (see Appendix 1), is essential. I also give the new owner the first few meals ready made-up, so that the first meals in strange surroundings taste exactly as what the puppy is used to. A warm blanket, which will smell familiar, is also provided.

If the puppy has had any of his inoculations, make sure that you

Ch. Ajestaweek Star Jester.

have the card from the vet duly filled in, so that the new veterinary surgeon will know precisely how much of the course of injections the pup has received. I always have Pet-Plan puppy cover for the first six weeks that they are away from home, which I pay, giving the cover note to the new owners along with the relevant leaflets on dog insurance so that they can take out permanent cover if they wish. This way I know that the pup is covered for veterinary attention and accidents should any mishap befall him on leaving home. I also insist on the puppy being returned to me if he is no longer wanted – at any time in his life. Finally one of the Bull Terrier Club early training leaflets goes with each pup, in the hope that it will smooth the path of both owner and puppy towards a contented relationship.

The character of the Bull Terrier is what first attracts those who love him – a legacy left by his ancestors, from whose lives of cruelty and stress sprang this faithful devotion and unwavering courage. These acknowledged and acclaimed qualities need to be perpetuated through the specialist breeders of today. Great as the glory surrounding the breed in the past has been, so much greater is the onus resting on the fancier of today to show himself capable of appreciating and maintaining the fine tradition entrusted in his hands in the form of the Bull Terrier.

(Bull Terrier Club Annual, 1937)

# Appendix 1

## Diet Sheet

### *8–20 Weeks    Four Meals a Day*

**Breakfast**  Weetabix or any cereal and brown bread or puppy meal in warm milk sweetened with a little glucose or honey.
**Lunch**  Half an ounce (12g) of meat per week of life, plus wholemeal puppy meal soaked in gravy or broth. Raw meat cut up small and fed warm. Add calcium and vitamin supplements.
**Tea**  A milk pudding, egg custard or the same as breakfast with added malt extract.
**Supper**  The same as lunch. Vary the meat – cooked or raw. In place of one meat meal use alternatively: one boiled or scrambled egg, a little grated cheese moistened with some raw egg or milk, fish, rabbit, chicken (well boned), or tripe (raw or cooked).

### *5–12 Months    Three Meals a Day*

Two big meals, plus a drink of milk and a few dry dog biscuits. No more than one pound (300g) of meat plus tablescraps for a pet. One and a half pounds (500g) of meat or more for a show dog.

### *Adults*

One pound (300g) or more of meat, plus biscuits. Calcium supplement. Malt extract. A Bull Terrier is a stong-boned dog and needs calcium to grow properly. A meaty marrow bone to gnaw right from the start helps the puppy to develop strong teeth, besides offering diversion and amusement. Always have a bowl of clean water within easy reach. A tin or pottery bowl is best as plastic ones can be chewed and the pieces can kill if swallowed.

# Appendix 2

## Insurance

The majority of breeders are now well aware of the hazards that face a carefully reared and nurtured puppy once he leaves home. However carefully the new owners have been selected there is no guarantee that every puppy will enjoy a trouble-free puppyhood. The first few weeks – while the puppy is adjusting to his new environment and the owners are getting used to having a puppy around – can be the most critical. By providing puppy insurance cover, you may not be able to prevent illness or accident but at least you can be confident that the new owners will be able to consult their vet at any time.

The puppy will be covered for the first six weeks away from his birthplace and the new owners will then be encouraged by the insurance company to take out permanent insurance for their pup. The scheme is very simple to operate. With a book of cover notes in the house, all that the breeder has to do is to complete the cover note, give the client the top copy and forward the duplicate to the insurance company together with the premium less the breeder's commission. The insurance takes effect as the new owners leave the breeder's premises and even provides cover during the journey to the new home.

Insurance to cover veterinary fees for an older dog is a very wise precaution. It means that a visit to the vet is not postponed because of the expense. So many things can go wrong and most of them are outside your control. Parvovirus, kennel cough, an accident or an attack by another dog, will all need veterinary attention.

This may seem a gloomy picture, but if you have adequate pet insurance at least it does not become a financial burden as well. I have had a dog eat her collar, including the buckle, another jam a piece of bone between her back teeth, another tear a schoolgirl's blazer. All were unexpected, but no financial worry.

179

There are several companies dealing in pet insurance, such as Prupet, Vetex, Pet Protect, Pet Guard and Dog Breeders' Insurance and Pet-Plan. Membership of Pro Dogs gives some insurance protection as does membership of some of the other canine societies and clubs. Pet-Plan offers a range of five plans. These are: puppy and kitten cover for the first six weeks away from their breeder, a show breeder policy for people who exhibit and/or breed dogs and cats, a boarding kennel plan to cover vets' fees whilst a pet is in kennels, quarantine for pets brought home from overseas, grooming, training and personal accident for those involved in services for pet owners. The variety of claims is enormous.

# Appendix 3

## Bull Terrier Rescue

As with any breed, there are times when, for reasons beyond anyone's control a dog has to be rehoused. It is a sad fact that once a Bull Terrier is passed to a new home he seems to pass through several homes. Many dogs are allowed to stray, some are dumped on the roadside because uncaring owners would rather go on holiday without them. Bull Terrier Clubs around the world endeavour to save these poor animals.

The Bull Terrier Club was the first pure breed club in great Britain to form its own rescue scheme. It was originally started privately and eventually the Bull Terrier Club stepped in to help with the costs. Miss Vick, of Rose Bungalow fame, took over the running of the Welfare for the Bull Terrier Club. Her kennels are situated in the south of England. For three years there was also a kennel in the north, working to assist with the ever increasing work-load but this system was being heavily overloaded with cases and the scheme was rapidly becoming financially ruinous to the Club. The Bull Terrier Club reformed the Welfare Scheme which came into operation on 1 September 1987.

The scheme makes use of two categories of volunteers: those who have a good understanding of the breed, are able to take a dog in for a few weeks, and are able to check his health and suitability for rehousing, and those who are able to collect and deliver dogs within an area specified by them and who are able to check prospective homes as to their suitability. All incoming Bull Terriers are kept for a minimum of two weeks in order to assess the dogs and to give owners a chance to reclaim them, or to make arrangements to house them. There is a Welfare Co-ordinator for the administration of the scheme and a Bull Terrier Club Welfare Scheme Standing Committee for the necessary policy decision making. Applicants for a Bull Terrier are visited by volunteers to check that the home is suitable.

With the increase in stealing and the dog fighting problems it is essential to check out every detail before rehousing a Bull Terrier, which has had one trauma already and does not need others. Funds to cover the expenses of the scheme are raised at various Exemption Shows and money-raising events throughout the year including a Grand Christmas Draw. Those receiving a Bull Terrier from the scheme are asked for a donation towards the cost of his sojourn amongst the volunteers. In the United States of America the American Bull Terrier Clubs in the various states run a rescue service or are affiliated to a rescue service for Bull Terriers.

# Appendix 4

## The Kennel Club of Great Britain Breed Standard

### *Bull Terrier*

*General Appearance* Strongly built, muscular, well balanced and active with a keen, determined and intelligent expression.

*Characteristics* The Bull Terrier is the gladiator of the canine race, full of fire and courageous. A unique feature is a downfaced, egg-shaped head. Irrespective of size dogs should look masculine and bitches feminine.

*Temperament* Of even temperament and amenable to discipline. Although obstinate is particularly good with people.

*Head and Skull* Head long, strong and deep right to end of muzzle, but not coarse. Viewed from front egg-shaped and completely filled, its surface free from hollows or identations. Top of skull almost flat from ear to ear. Profile curves gently downwards from top of skull to tip of nose which should be black and bent downwards at tip. Nostrils well developed and underjaw deep and strong.

*Mouth* Teeth sound, clean, strong, of good size, perfectly regular with a perfect regular and complete scissor bite, i.e. upper teeth closely overlapping lower teeth and set square to the jaws. Lips clean and tight.

*Eyes* Appearing narrow, obliquely placed and triangular, well sunken, black or as dark brown as possible so as to appear almost black, and with a piercing glint. Distance from tip of nose to eyes perceptibly greater than that from eyes to top of skull. Blue or partly blue undesirable.

*Ears* Small, thin and placed close together. Dog should be able to hold them stiffly erect, when they point straight upwards.

*Neck* Very muscular, long, arched, tapering from shoulders to head and free from loose skin.

*Forequarters* Shoulders strong and muscular without loading. Shoulder blades wide, flat and held closely to chest wall and have a very pronounced backward slope of front edge from bottom to top, forming almost a right angle with upper arm. Elbows held straight and strong, pasterns upright. Forelegs have strongest type of round, quality bone, dog should stand solidly upon them and they should be perfectly parallel. In mature dogs length of foreleg should be approximately equal to depth of chest.

*Body* Body well rounded with marked spring of rib and great depth from withers to brisket, so that latter nearer ground than belly. Back short, strong with backline behind withers level, arching or roaching, slightly over broad, well muscled loins. Underline from brisket to belly forms a graceful upward curve. Chest broad when viewed from front.

*Hindquarters* Hindlegs in parallel when viewed from behind. Thighs muscular and second thighs well developed. Stifle joint well bent and hock well angulated with bone to foot short and strong.

*Feet* Round and compact with well arched toes.

*Tail* Short, set on low and carried horizontally. Thick at root, it tapers to a fine point.

*Gait/Movement* When moving appears well knit, smoothly covering ground with free, easy strides and with a typical jaunty air. When trotting, movement parallel, front and back, only converging towards centre line at faster speeds, forelegs reaching out well and hindlegs moving smoothly at hip, flexing well at stifle and hock, with great thrust.

*Coat* Short, flat, even and harsh to touch with a fine gloss. Skin fitting dog tightly. A soft textured undercoat may be present in winter.

*Colour* For White, pure white coat. Skin pigmentation and markings on head not to be penalised. For Coloured, colour predominates, all others things being equal, brindle preferred. Black brindle, red, fawn and tri-colour acceptable. Tick markings in white coat undesirable. Blue and liver highly undesirable.

*Size* There are neither weight nor height limits, but there should be the impression of maximum substance for size of dog consistent with quality and sex.

*Faults* Any departure from the foregoing points should be considered a fault and the seriousness with which the fault should be regarded should be in exact proportion to its degree.

*Note* Male animals should have two apparently normal testicles fully descended into the scrotum.

## Bull Terrier (Miniature)

The Standard of the Bull Terrier (Miniature) is the same as that of the Bull Terrier with the exception of the following:

*Size* Height should not exceed 14in (35.5cm). There should be an impression of substance to size of dog. There is no weight limit. Dog should at all times be balanced.

# The American Kennel Club Breed Standard

## White

The Bull Terrier must be strongly built, muscular, symmetrical and active, with a keen, determined and intelligent expression, full of fire but of sweet disposition and amenable to discipline.
  *The head* should be long, strong and deep right to the end of the

muzzle, but not coarse. Full face it should be oval in outline and be filled completely up giving the impression of fullness with a surface devoid of hollows or indentations, i.e. egg shaped. In profile it should curve gently downwards from the top of the skull to the tip of the nose. The forehead should be flat across from ear to ear. The distance from the tip of the nose to the eyes should be perceptibly greater than that from the eyes to the top of the skull. The underjaw should be deep and well defined. *The lips* should be clean and tight. *The teeth* should meet in either a level or in a scissors bite. In the scissors bite the upper teeth should fit in front of and closely against the lower teeth, and they should be sound, strong and perfectly regular.

*The ears* should be small, thin and placed close together. They should be capable of being held stiffly erect, when they should point upwards. *The eyes* should be well sunken and as dark as possible, with a piercing glint and they should be small, triangular and obliquely placed; set near together and high up on the dog's head. Blue eyes are a disqualification. *The nose* should be black, with well-developed nostrils bent downward at the tip.

*The neck* should be very muscular, long, arched and clean, tapering from the shoulders to the head and should be free from loose skin. *The chest* should be broad when viewed from in front, and there should be great depth from withers to brisket, so that the latter is nearer the ground than the belly.

*The body* should be well rounded with marked spring of rib, the back should be short and strong. The back ribs deep, slightly arched over the loin. The shoulders should be strong and muscular but without heaviness. The shoulder blades should be wide and flat and there should be a very pronounced backward slope from the bottom edge of the blade to the top edge. Behind the shoulders there should be no slackness or dip at the withers. The underline from the brisket to the belly should form a graceful upward curve.

*The legs* should be big boned but not to the point of coarseness; the forelegs should be of moderate length, perfectly straight, and the dog must stand firmly upon them. The elbows must turn neither in nor out, and the pasterns should be strong and upright. The hind legs should be parallel viewed from behind. The thighs very muscular with hocks well let down. Hind pasterns short and upright. The stifle joint should be well bent with a well-developed second thigh. *The feet* round and compact with well-arched toes like a cat.

*The tail* should be short, set on low, fine, and ideally should be carried horizontally. It should be thick where it joins the body, and should taper to a fine point.

*The coat* should be short, flat, harsh to the touch and with a fine gloss. The dog's skin should fit tightly. *The colour* is white though markings on the head are permissible. Any markings elsewhere on the coat are to be severely faulted. Skin pigmentation is not to be penalised.

*Movement* – the dog shall move smoothly, covering the ground with free, easy strides, fore and hind legs should move parallel each to each when viewed from in front or behind. The forelegs reaching out well and the hind legs moving smoothly at the hip and flexing well at the stifle and hock. The dog should move compactly and in one piece but with a typical jaunty air that suggests agility and power.

## Faults

Any departure from the foregoing points shall be considered a fault and the seriousness of the fault shall be in exact proportion to its degree, i.e. a very crooked front is a very bad fault; a rather crooked front is a rather bad fault and a slightly crooked front is a slight fault.

## Disqualification

Blue eyes.

## Coloured

The Standard for the Coloured Variety is the same as for the White except for the subhead 'Colour' which reads: *Colour.* Any colour other than white, or any colour with white markings. Other things being equal, the preferred colour is brindle. A dog which is predominantly white shall be disqualified.

## Disqualifications

Blue eyes.
Any dog which is predominantly white.

*Approved 9 July 1974*

# Bibliography

Bush, Barry, BVSc., Phd., FRCVS, *Dog Care* (Orbis Publishing, 1982)

Harmer, Hilary, *Dogs and How to Breed Them* (John Gifford Ltd., 1968)

Horner, T.J., *All About the Bull Terrier* (Pelham Books, 1973)
   *Terriers of the World, Their History and Characteristics* (Faber and Faber, 1984)
   *The Souperlative Story* (B.T.C., 1987)

Lorenz, Konrad, *Man Meets Dog* (Methuen, 1954)

Oppenheimer, R.H., *McGuffin & Co.* (Dogworld, 1964)
   *After Bar Sinister* (Dogworld, 1964)

Rubin, S., DVM, *Emergency and First Aid for Dogs* (Fredrick Muller Ltd., 1982)

*The Bull Terrier Club Handbook*

*The Bull Terrier Club Sixth Book*

*Bull Terrier Tales* Weeks, M.R. (ed.),(B.T.C., 1988)

189

# Index

age, of bitch: and mating, 130–1
aggressiveness, 26, 131, 132
American Pit Bull Terrier, 7
anatomy: of dog, 126–7
awards, system of, 115–16

back: shape of, 21
baths, 90, 142
bed: dog, 32–3, 174
　'vet', 33
bedding, 33, 38, 142, 148
behaviour: and whelping, 150–2, 155
Best: of Breed, 75, 106, 114
　in Show, 76, 82, 101, 106
bitch: and breeding, 122–3
　brood, 128–31, 139
　care of, 169–70
　maiden, 131, 155
　mating, 131
　in season, 122, 127
　　signs of, 128
　see also under pregnancy
bite: types of, 17–19
block chalk: use of, 90
bones: dangers of, 35
breath: and diet, 51
　and teeth, 68
Breed Standard, 11, 12, 15, 72
　of American Kennel Club, 186–8
　faults, 187–8
　judging to, 113
breeders, 9, 11, 28, 39, 72, 117
　as judges, 113
　reliability of, 29, 118, 123
　visits to, 30
breeding, 117–31
　arrangements for, 122–3
　inter–, 118

line–, 118–19, 120–21
breeds: of Bull Terriers, 7
Bull Terrier:
　care of older dog, 67–71
　mature, 60–72
　as member of family, 50, 60
　as mothers, 158–9
　owning more than one, 60–6
　points of, 12
　in show-ring, 103–12
　skeleton, 13, 187
　and whelping, 138
Bull Terrier Club, 8, 9, 29, 38, 138
　Rescue, 182–3
　shows, 29, 115
　Welfare Scheme, 74, 80, 182
Bull Terrier Club of America, 29

Caesarian section, 161
cage, dog, 32, 44–5, 62, 97–8
　for show bench, 92, 100
　travelling, 33, 38, 45, 97
　in whelping box, 146, 174
cardboard box, for whelping, 153–4
cards, place, 77, 115
Challenge certificates, 74, 76–8, 85–6,
　113–15
Champion Bull Terriers, 109–11
Championship shows, 74–6, 78, 80–2,
　85–6, 97, 105, 116
characteristics, 7, 25–7, 60, 177
　variety of, 29–30
children: and Bull Terriers, 27, 44
classes, in shows, 84–6
　Kennel Club, 73, 75
　records of, 86
cleanliness, 36–7, 142
cleft palates, 120

190

coat, 24, 90, 121, 124, 170
collars, 37, 46, 47, 57, 94–5, 156
colour, of Bull Terriers, 7, 8, 24–5,
    187–8
  breeding, 120–1, 122
  of eyes, 14–15
  of nose, 19
  'solids', 24
  –vision, 14
commands, 34, 46, 53–6
conformation: of Bull Terriers, 11–27
costs: of breeding, 117
  of showing, 77–80
cross-breeding, 7
Cruft's, 9, 74, 76, 85, 92, 116
cryptorchid, 126

deafness, 121, 171–2
diet, 67, 69, 70, 71, 124, 140–1, 161–2
  sheet, 38, 40, 171, 176, 179

ears, 15, 68, 171–2, 186
  cleanliness, 50–1, 67–8, 91
  cropping of, 8–9
  taping, 51–3
eclampsia, 141, 152, 161
entry: to show, 82–7, 100, 102
environment: stress of, 41, 49
exemption shows, 73–4, 77, 84
eyes, 13–15, 68, 172, 186
  cleanliness, 51, 91
  colour of, 14–15
  shape of, 14, 31

feeding, 33–4, 40, 164–8
feet, 22, 91, 187
fighting, 62–6
  dog–, practice of, 62–3, 183
  by puppies, 174–5
food, 140–1
  and commands, 54
  for puppies, 165–6

genes: and breeding, 118
gestation tables: canine, 142
grooming, 45, 50–3, 142
  for show, 90–2

handling, 88
  of puppies, 42–3, 170, 173
head, 11, 186
  shape of, 12–13
heart: problems of, 69
hindquarters, 22, 23
hormone imbalance: of bitch, 170
house training, 40–4

identity discs, 37, 47
inoculations, 34, 37, 43, 48, 49, 124,
    176–7
insurance: dog, 177, 180–1

jaws, 16, 35, 105
  see also overshot; undershot
judges: types of, 112–13
judging, 104–5, 113–14

kennel, 36–7, 50
  staff, 80
Kennel Club, 8, 9, 11
  classes, 73, 75, 82
  Registration papers, 38, 123, 176
  rules, 82, 106
  and shows, 73, 116
kidney failure, 70

lamp: infra-red, for whelping, 148–9
lapping: learning to, 164–5
leads, 37, 46, 47–8, 57–8, 64, 66, 87, 89
  types of, 93–4
legs: proportion of, 22, 187
litters: number of, 131
  size of, 117

malt extract: use of, 34, 46, 179
mastitis, 162
mating, 122, 128, 130–7
mealtimes, 170–1
medical: care, 34
  supplies, for whelping, 154
metritis, 162–3
milk: after whelping, 162, 165, 170
monorchid, 115, 126
mouth, 15–19, 31, 105, 114
movement, 25, 105–6, 114, 187
muzzle, 15, 31

muzzling: in mating, 131, 133–5

nails, 103
  filing, 50, 67, 91, 124, 169
name, 46, 58
  registered, 82–3
neck, 20, 186
nervousness, 30, 41, 132, 133
newspaper: use of, 35, 37, 40–1, 59,
  154
noise, 41, 88
nose, 19, 103, 186

obedience training, 49, 66–7
odour: from bitch, 128, 130
open shows, 74, 80–1, 84–6, 104,
  108–12
out crosses, 119–20
overshot jaw, 19, 31, 157

pacing: habit of, 25
pack leaders, 26, 27, 48, 60, 62–3
pedigree, 29, 38, 118, 123, 176
pig rail, 145–6, 147, 165
pincer bite, 17, 19
play, 44, 61, 174
  pen, 169, 173–4
possessiveness, 59
pregnancy, 138–52
  false, 143
preparation: for show, 87–96
  for whelping, 153–4
puppy, 28–39, 62, 84
  integration by, 172–5
  new home for, 175–7

rearing: of puppies, 164–77
records: of shows, 112
reproductive organs, 127, 129
ring: show, 101, 103–12
ringcraft, 66, 87–90
run: cleanliness of, 36–7

schedule: of show, 76, 82
showground, 97–103
  plan of, 99
showing, 66, 72–81
shows, 72, 97–116
  choice of, 76–8
  types of, 73–5, 76, 102
skin, 24, 69
socialisation, 40–9, 66, 164
Staffordshire Bull Terrier, 62
stifle joint, 22, 23, 24, 30
stop, the, 13, 31
stride: length of, 21, 25, 114
stud: –book, 85, 124
  card, 125
  dog, 118–27

tail: carriage of, 22–3, 89, 187
  curling, by bitch, 128, 129
  trimming, 92, 103
teeth, 15–17, 105, 106, 113, 114, 171,
  186
  cleaning, 51, 68, 91
temperament, 25–7, 28, 60, 122
theft: of Bull Terriers, 36, 62, 92, 183
  at shows, 98, 100, 103, 107
tie: in mating, 126, 134, 136
training, 38, 46–9, 50–9, 60, 87–90
travel: and dogs, 38, 79, 81, 98

unbenched shows, 75, 102, 104
undershot jaw, 15, 17–19, 31, 157

veterinary surgeons, 34, 45, 155, 180
vitamin supplements, 34, 67, 140–1
voice: tone of, 59, 60, 88

walking: to heel, 48, 87–90
walks, 43, 61, 67
weaning, 164–7
whelping, 123, 131, 138, 142–8,
  153–63, 174
whiskers: trimming, 92, 102
worming, 51, 168–9